PHILIP'S ESSENTIAL SCHOOL ATLAS

Published in Great Britain in 2016 by Philip's,
a division of Octopus Publishing Group Limited
(www.octopusbooks.co.uk)
Carmelite House, 50 Victoria Embankment
London EC4Y 0DZ
An Hachette UK Company
(www.hachette.co.uk)

Printed in Hong Kong

Cartography by Philip's
Previously published as
Philip's Student Atlas

Copyright © 2016 Philip's

HARDBACK EDITION
ISBN 978-1-84907-406-3

PAPERBACK EDITION
ISBN 978-1-84907-407-0

SUBJECT LIST

Details of other Philip's titles and services can be found on our website at:
www.philips-maps.co.uk

MAP SYMBOLS

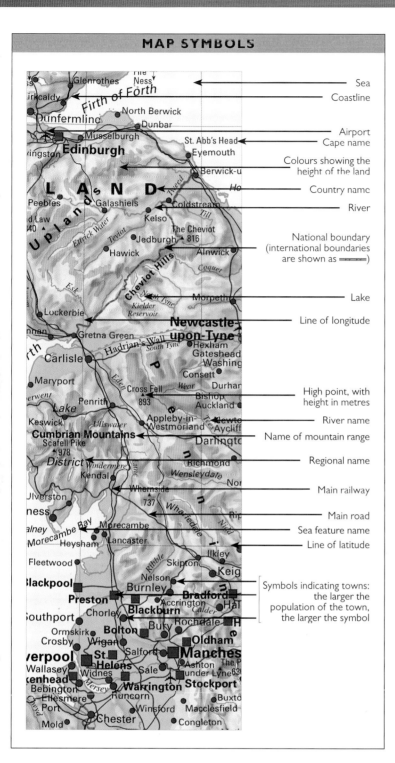

- Sea
- Coastline
- Airport
- Cape name
- Colours showing the height of the land
- Country name
- River
- National boundary (international boundaries are shown as ▬ ▬ ▬)
- Lake
- Line of longitude
- High point, with height in metres
- River name
- Name of mountain range
- Regional name
- Main railway
- Main road
- Sea feature name
- Line of latitude
- Symbols indicating towns: the larger the population of the town, the larger the symbol

HEIGHT OF LAND

There is an explanation like this one on every page where different colours are used to show the height of the land above sea level.

The highest point in a region is shown with the symbol ▲ plus the height in metres.

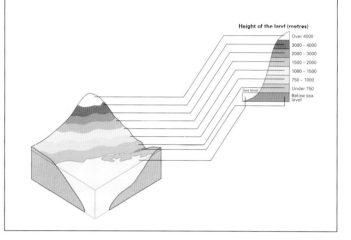

Height of the land (metres)

Over 4000 / 3000 – 4000 / 2000 – 3000 / 1500 – 2000 / 1000 – 1500 / 750 – 1000 / Under 750 / Below sea level / Sea level

SCALE BAR

Every map has a scale statement, scale bar and ruler accompanying it. For a full explanation of scale and how to use the scale bar, see page 2.

Scale 1:48 000 000   1 cm on the map = 480 km on the ground

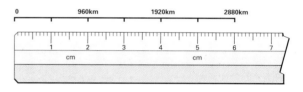

SCALE COMPARISON MAP

This map, or one of the U.K. and Ireland, appears on most of the maps of the continents at the same scale as the main map. They give an idea of the size of that continent.

England and Wales on same scale

LOCATOR MAP

There is a small map such as this on every map page. The bright green area shows how the main map fits into its larger region.

Philip's World Atlases are published in association with The Royal Geographical Society (with The Institute of British Geographers).

The Society was founded in 1830 and given a Royal Charter in 1859 for 'the advancement of geographical science'. Today it is a leading world centre for geographical learning – supporting education, teaching, research and expeditions, and promoting public understanding of the subject.

Further information about the Society and how to join may be found on its website at: **www.rgs.org**

PHOTOGRAPHIC ACKNOWLEDGEMENTS
Alamy /Roger Bamber p. 24 (centre), /Stocktrek Images, Inc. p. 36; **Corbis** /Tim Graham p. 24 (bottom), /Reuters p. 44, /Royalty Free p. 73; **Crown Copyright** p. 7 (map extract); **Eurostar** p. 26; **Fotolia.co.uk** p. 76; **NPA Satellite Mapping** pp. 8, 9, 10, 12, 26, 27, 37, 49, 60, 61, 74, 78, 79; **iStockphoto.com** p. 24 (top); **Patricia and Angus Macdonald** p. 7; **NASA** p. 11; **Precision Terrain Surveys Ltd** p. 6.

Ordnance Survey   Page 6: The Edinburgh city plan is based on mapping data licensed from Ordnance Survey® with the permission of the Controller of Her Majesty's Stationery Office. © Crown copyright 2016. All rights reserved. Licence number 100011710.

Scale and Direction

TYPES OF SCALE

In this atlas the scale of the map is shown in three ways:

WRITTEN STATEMENT

This tells you how many kilometres on the Earth are represented by one centimetre on the map.

1 cm on the map = 20 km on the ground

SCALE RATIO

This tells you that one unit on the map represents two million of the same unit on the ground.

Scale 1:2 000 000

SCALE BAR

This shows you the scale as a line or bar with a section of ruler beneath it.

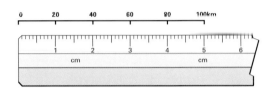

HOW TO MEASURE DISTANCE

The map on the right is a small part of the map of Southern Europe, which is on page 34 in the World section of the atlas.

The scale of the map extract is shown below:

Scale 1:10 000 000   1 cm on the map = 100 km on the ground

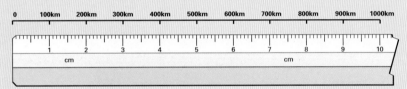

To measure the distance from London to Paris you can use any of the three methods described above.

For example:

USING THE WRITTEN STATEMENT

Using the scale above, you can see that 1 centimetre on the map represents 100 kilometres on the ground.

Measure the distance on the map between London and Paris. You will see that this is about 3.5 centimetres.

If 1 cm = 100 km

then 3.5 cm = 350 km (3.5 x 100)

USING THE SCALE RATIO

Using the scale above, you can see that the ratio is 1:10 000 000.

We know that the distance on the map between the cities is 3.5 cm and we know from the ratio that 1 cm on the map = 10 000 000 cm on the ground.

We multiply the map distance by the ratio.

= 3.5 x 10 000 000 cm
= 35 000 000 cm
= 350 000 m
= 350 km

USING THE SCALE BAR

We know that the distance on the map between the cities is 3.5 centimetres.

Measure 3.5 cm along the scale bar (or use the ruler as a guide) and read off the distance in kilometres.

Using these three methods, now work out the distance between London and Cardiff on the map above.

The map on the left is an extract from the map of Asia on page 39 in the World section of the atlas. Below, you can see the scale of this map. See if you can calculate the distance between Kolkata and Bangkok.

Scale 1:48 000 000   1 cm on the map = 480 km on the ground

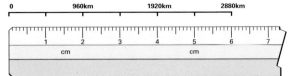

DIFFERENT SIZES OF SCALE

The table on the right shows the distances from London to Paris and Bangkok to Kolkata on the maps on page 2. The map distances are both 3.5 centimetres, but the distances on the ground are very different. This is because the maps are at different scales.

Included on most of the continent maps, in the World section of this atlas, are **scale comparison maps**. These show you the size of the UK and Ireland, or England and Wales, drawn at the same scale as the main map on that page. This is to give you an idea of the size of that continent.

	Map Distance	Map Scale	Distance on the Ground
London – Paris	3.5 centimetres	1:10 000 000	350 kilometres
Bangkok – Kolkata	3.5 centimetres	1:48 000 000	1,680 kilometres

Below are three maps which appear in this atlas:

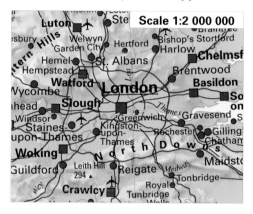

Scale 1:2 000 000

Scale 1:7 500 000

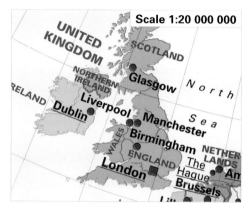

Scale 1:20 000 000

These maps all show London, but the map above shows much more detail than the maps on the right. The map above is a larger-scale map than the maps on the right.

A **large-scale** map shows more detail of a **small** area.

A **small-scale** map shows less detail of a **large** area.

Notice how the scale ratios at the top right of each map are getting larger as the scale of the map gets smaller.

DIRECTION ON THE MAPS

On most of the atlas maps, north is at the top of the page. Lines of latitude cross the maps from east to west. Longitude lines run from south to north. These usually curve a little because the Earth is a globe and not a flat shape.

POINTS OF THE COMPASS

Below is a drawing of the points of a compass. North, east, south and west are called **cardinal points**. Direction is sometimes given in degrees. This is measured clockwise from north. To help you remember the order of the compass points, try to learn this sentence:

Naughty **E**lephants **S**quirt **W**ater

USING A COMPASS

Compasses have a needle with a magnetic tip. The tip is attracted towards the Magnetic North Pole, which is close to the Geographical North Pole. The compass tells you where north is. You can see the Magnetic North Pole on the diagram below.

ACTIVITIES

Look at the map below.
If Ambleside is east of Belfast then:

- Valencia is _____ of Belfast;
- Renfrew is _____ of Ambleside;
- Oxford is _____ of Plymouth;
- Belfast is _____ of Oxford;
- Plymouth is _____ of Renfrew.

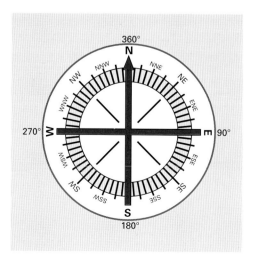

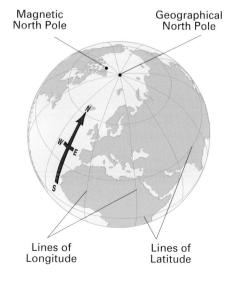

Magnetic North Pole   Geographical North Pole

Lines of Longitude   Lines of Latitude

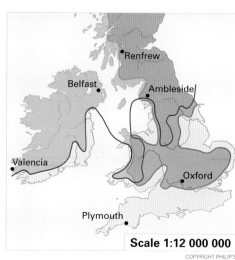

Scale 1:12 000 000

LATITUDE

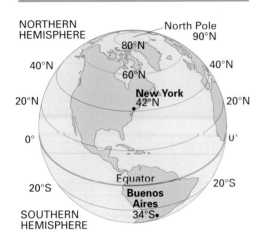

LONGITUDE

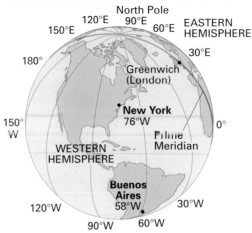

USING LATITUDE & LONGITUDE

Lines of latitude cross the atlas maps from east to west. The **Equator** is at 0°. All other lines of latitude are either north of the Equator, or south of the Equator. Line 40°N is almost halfway towards the North Pole. The North Pole is at 90°N. At the Equator, a degree of longitude measures about 110 km.

Lines of longitude run from north to south. These lines meet at the North Pole and the South Pole. Longitude 0° passes through Greenwich. This line is also called the Prime Meridian. Lines of longitude are either east of 0° or west of 0°. There are 180 degrees of longitude both east and west of 0°.

There are 60 minutes in a degree. Latitude and longitude lines make a grid. You can find a place if you know its latitude and longitude number. The latitude number is either north or south of the Equator. The longitude number is either east or west of the Greenwich Meridian.

SPECIAL LATITUDE LINES

The Earth's axis is tilted at an angle of approximately 23½°. In June, the northern hemisphere is tilted towards the Sun. On 21 June the Sun is directly overhead at the **Tropic of Cancer**, 23°26'N, and this is midsummer in the northern hemisphere. Midsummer in the southern hemisphere occurs on 21 December, when the Sun is overhead at the **Tropic of Capricorn**, 23°26'S. On the maps in this atlas these are shown as blue dotted lines.

In the North and South Polar regions there are places where the Sun does not rise or set above the horizon at certain times of the year. These places are also shown by a blue dotted line on the maps. The **Arctic Circle** is at 66°34'N and the **Antarctic Circle** is at 66°34'S.

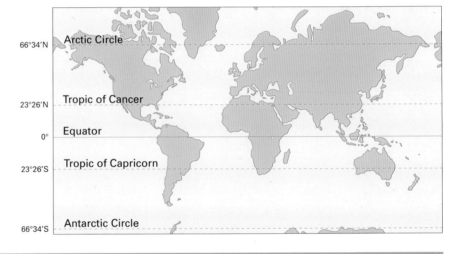

LATITUDE AND LONGITUDE IN THIS ATLAS

In this atlas lines of latitude and longitude are coloured blue.

On large-scale maps, such as those of England and Wales on pages 16–17, there is a line for every degree. On smaller-scale maps only every other, every fifth or even tenth line is shown.

The map on the right shows the UK and Ireland. The latitude and longitude lines are numbered at the edges of the map. The bottom of the map shows whether a place is east or west of Greenwich. The side of the map tells you how far north from the Equator the line is.

Around the edges of the map are small yellow pointers with letters or figures in their boxes. Columns made by longitude lines have letters in their boxes; rows made by latitude lines have figures.

In the index at the end of the atlas, places have figure-letter references as well as latitude and longitude numbers to help you locate the place names on the maps.

On the map opposite, London is in rectangle **8M** (this is where row 8 crosses with column M). Edinburgh is in **4J** and Dublin is in **6F**.

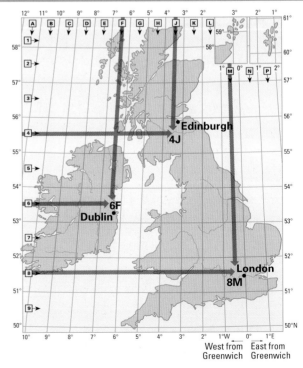

HOW TO FIND A PLACE

The map on the right is an extract from the map of Scotland on page 18. If you want to find Stornoway in the atlas, you must look in the index. Places are listed alphabetically. You will find the following entry:

Stornoway .... 58° 13'N 6° 23'W **18 1B**

The first number in **bold** type is the page number where the map appears. The figure and letter which follow the page number give the grid rectangle on the map in which the feature appears. Here we can see that Stornoway is on page 18 in the rectangle where row 1 crosses column B.

The latitude and longitude number corresponds with the numbered lines on the map. The first set of figures represent the latitude and the second set represent the longitude. The unit of measurement for latitude and longitude is the degree (°) which is divided into minutes (').

Latitude and longitude can be used to locate places more accurately on smaller-scale maps such as those in the World section. A more detailed explanation of how to estimate the minutes can be found on page 90.

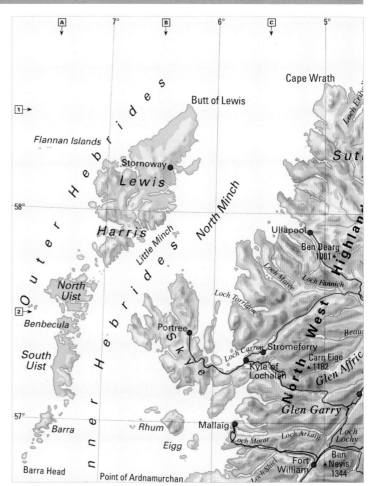

MAKING MAPS

One of the greatest problems in making maps is how to draw the curved surface of the globe on a flat piece of paper. As a globe is three dimensional, it is not possible to show its surface on a flat map without some form of distortion.

This map (right) shows one way of putting the globe on to paper, but because it splits up the land and sea it is not very useful.

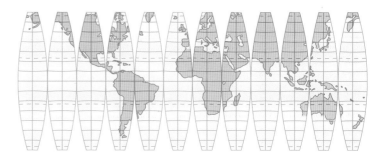

The map below is better because it shows the correct size of places. It is an **equal-area map**. For example, Australia is the correct size in relation to North America, and Europe is the correct size in relation to Africa. Comparing certain areas is a useful way to check the accuracy of maps. Comparing Greenland (2.2 million km²) with Australia (7.7 million km²) is a good 'area test'.

The map below is called **Mercator**. It has been used since the 16th century. The area scale is not equal area, but many sea and air routes are drawn on this type of map because direction is accurate. The scale of distances is difficult to put on a world map. On the Mercator map, scale is correct along the Equator but is less correct towards the Poles.

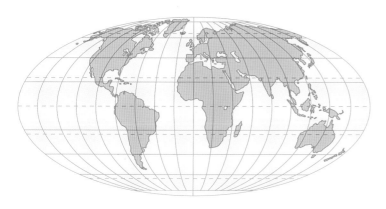

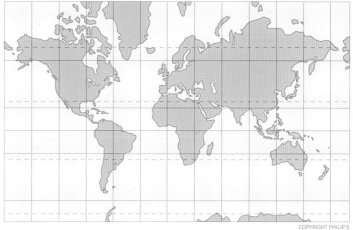

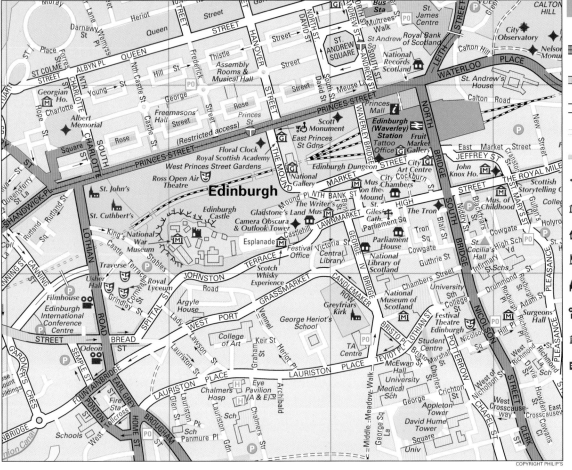

KEY TO MAP SYMBOLS

- Main Road Dual
- Secondary Road Single
- Minor Road
- → One Way Street
- Pedestrian Roads
- ✝ Abbey/Cathedral
- 🏛 Art Gallery
- 🏛 Building of Public Interest
- 🏰 Castle
- ⛪ Church of interest
- 🎥 Cinema
- 🏛 Museum
- 🚉 Railway Station

- Shopping Street
- 🚊 Tram Route with Station
- ┅┅ Railway
- Railway / Bus Station
- Shopping Precinct / Retail Park
- Park
- 🎭 Theatre
- ℹ️ Tourist Information Centre
- ◆ Other Place Interest
- Ⓗ Hospital
- Ⓟ Parking
- PO Post Office
- ▲ Youth Hostel

Edinburgh

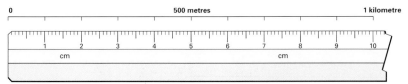

Scale 1:10 000 1 centimetre on the map and aerial photograph = 100 metres on the ground

```
0                    500 metres                 1 kilometre

1    2    3    4    5    6    7    8    9    10
   cm                        cm
```

Locator map

Edinburgh

St Ives

KEY TO MAP SYMBOLS

A 30	Main road		Other road, drive or track, fenced and unfenced
B 3074	Secondary road		Path
	Road generally more than 4m wide		Footpath
	Road generally less than 4m wide		National Trail/ Long Distance Route; Recreation Route
	Single track		Cutting; tunnel; embankment
	Road over; Road under; Level crossing;		Station, open to passengers; siding
	Coniferous trees		Scrub
	non-coniferous trees		Bracken, heath or rough grassland
	Coppice		Slopes

Place of worship

ent or former e or worship { with tower / with spire, minaret or dome

CH Clubhouse
FB Footbridge
PO Post office
Sch School

Building; important building

Lighthouse, disused lighthouse; beacon

Triangulation pillar; mast

W; Spr Well; spring

Ground survey height
Air survey height

Surface heights are to the nearest metre above mean sea level. Where two heights are shown, the first height is to the base of the triangulation pillar and the second (in brackets) to the highest natural point of the hill

Vertical face/cliff

Contours may be at 5 or 10 metres vertical interval

Parking/Park & Ride, all year/seasonal — Camp site/caravan site

Information centre, all year/seasonal — Recreation/leisure/ sports centre

Museum — Golf course or links

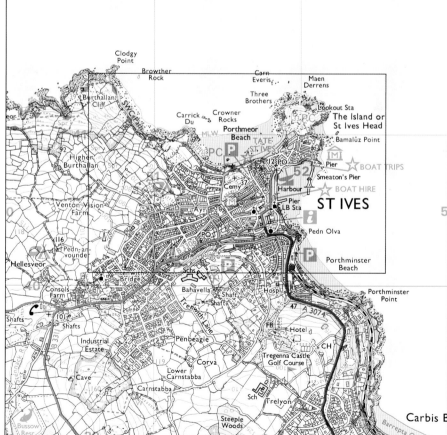

Reproduced from the 2008 Ordnance Survey 1:25,000 Explorer Map with permission of the controller of Her Majesty's Stationery office © Crown Copyright

cale of photograph 1:10 000

500 metres

centimetre on the photograph = 100 metres on the ground

Scale of map 1:25 000

0   500 metres   1 km   1.5 kilometres

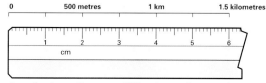

1 centimetre on the map = 250 metres on the ground

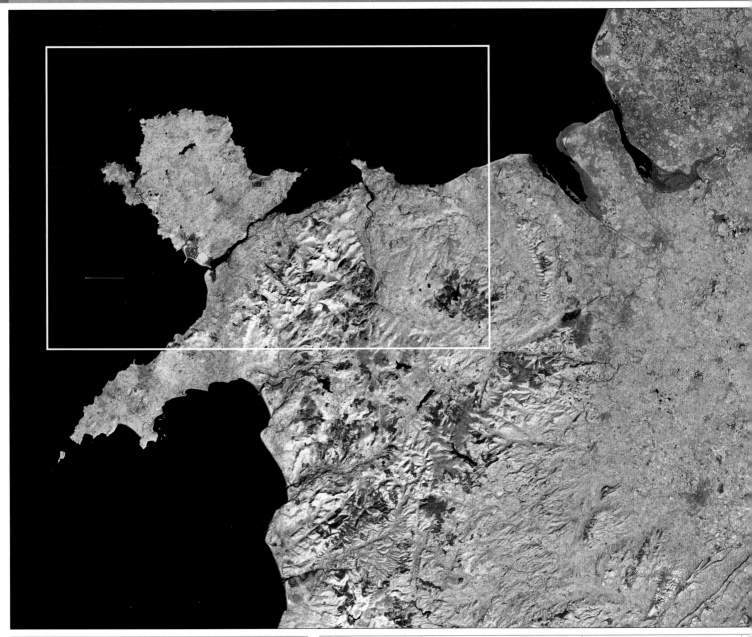

KEY TO MAP SYMBOLS

⊙ ◉ ◉ ◉ ◎ ⊙ ○ ○ Town symbols

▱	Built-up areas	———————	Main passenger railways
CONWY	Administrative area names	———————	Other passenger railways
SNOWDONIA	National park names	⊕	Major airports
═══════	Motorways	∿	Rivers
———————	Major roads	▱	Lakes or reservoirs
———————	Other important roads	▲ 1085	Elevations in metres
———————	Administrative boundaries	■	Places of interest

Locator map

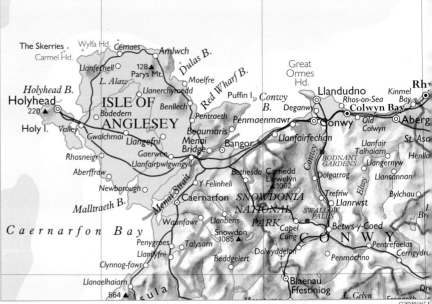

Scale 1:760 000 1 cm on the map and satellite image = 7.6 km on the ground

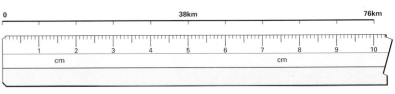

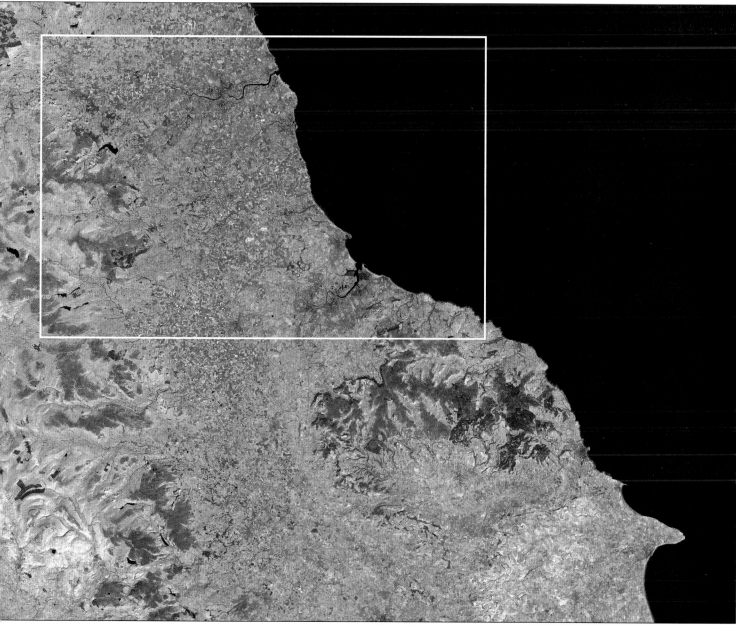

SATELLITE IMAGERY

images on these pages were produced by the
...dsat 7 satellite, launched by NASA in 1999.
...avels around the Earth at a height of over
... km. It is able to scan every part of the Earth's
...face once every 16 days. The data is
...smitted back to Earth where it is printed in
...e colours to make certain features stand out.
...n these pages grass and crops appear light
...en, soils and exposed rock light grey, woodland
...: green, moorland brown, water black and
...t-up areas dark grey. The image on this page
...ws North-east England and the image on page
...ows North Wales. Both images were
...rded in late March. Comparing the maps,
...ch are taken from *Philip's Modern School Atlas*
... the images helps identify specific features on
...mages.

Locator map

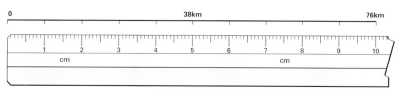

Scale 1:760 000   1 cm on the map and satellite image = 7.6 km on the ground

| 0 | 38km | 76km |

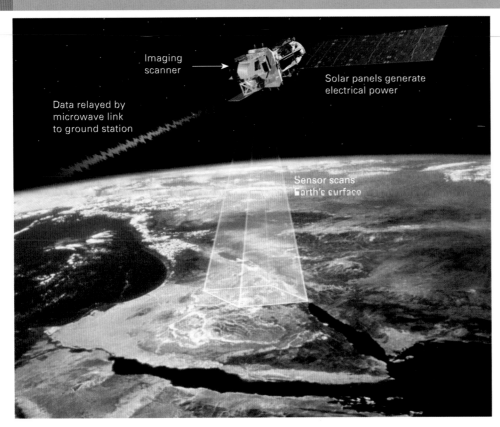

Imaging scanner

Solar panels generate electrical power

Data relayed by microwave link to ground station

Sensor scans Earth's surface

◀ Earth Observation Satellites

Powered by outstretched solar panels, Earth Observation Satellites, such as the one shown here, can collect and relay back to Earth huge volumes of geographical data which is then processed and stored on computers.

Depending on the sensors fitted, the choice of orbit and altitude, these satellites can provide detailed imagery of the Earth's surface at close range or monitor environmental issues covering the entire world. Objects less than 1 metre across can now be seen from space as well as the entire surface of our planet, allowing us to monitor issues such as the atmosphere, land and sea temperature, vegetation, rainfall and ice cover.

The importance of recording this information over time is that it enables us to see long-term changes and increases our understanding of the processes involved. Some satellites have been collecting data for over 25 years. A few of their uses are shown on this page and the page opposite.

▲ The River Thames, London

This image shows central London from St Paul's Cathedral, in the upper left-hand corner, across to the Tower of London and Tower Bridge on the right-hand side. The image was captured from a satellite 680 km above the Earth and travelling at 6 km per second. It was captured at about midday in late October, the low sun showing clearly the shadows of the Shard and the chimney of Tate Modern. (Image © EUSI, Inc. All Rights Reserved/NPA Satellite Mapping)

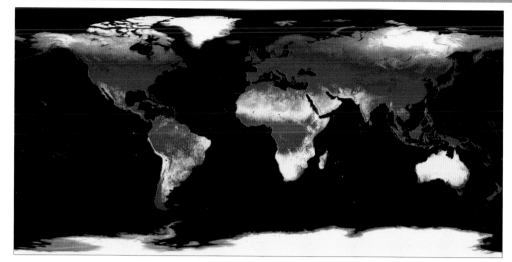

◄ World Land Surface Temperature, November 2012
The satellite which captured this data uses another set of sensors that enable it to capture different data and over a much wider area. The colours range from light blue, indicating −25°C, through reds and oranges up to yellow, indicating +45°C. The land surface temperature thus shows the beginning of winter north of the Equator and summer south of the Equator.

▲ Alexander Island, Antarctica
An important use for satellites is to monitor inaccessible areas of the world that are environmentally sensitive, such as the ice caps surrounding the North and South Poles. This image shows the Hampton Glacier, which is at the foot of the image, flowing towards the sea. The ice then breaks off into a series of icebergs, which can be seen at the top. Because satellites revisit these areas regularly, changes to the extent of the ice can be monitored.

▲ Weather
Weather satellites travel at the same speed as the Earth's rotation and stay in daylight to allow them to monitor the same area for major storms and other events. In order to capture as much of the Earth's surface as possible, they orbit farther out in space, about 35,000 km above the Earth's surface. This image clearly shows a hurricane approaching the coast of central America and the Gulf of Mexico.

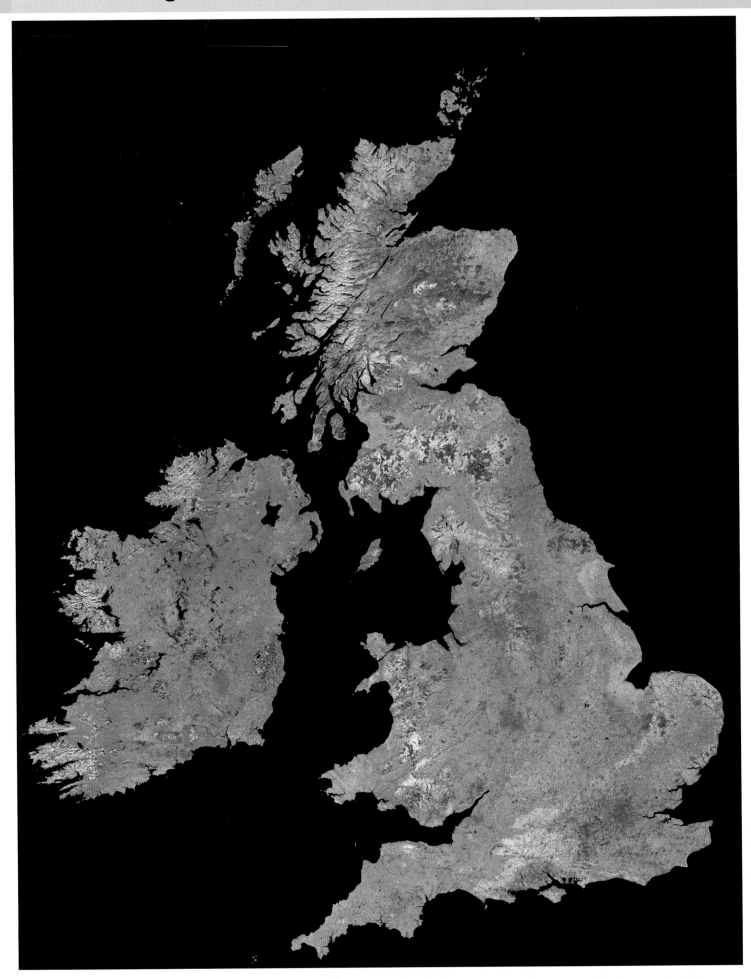

▲ **The United Kingdom and Ireland, seen from Space**

The colours on this image have been processed to match the natural tone of the landscape. The large amount of agricultural land in the UK is reflected by the extensive green on the image. In Scotland, the snow-covered Cairngorm Mountains can be seen, with brownish-green coniferous forests below the snow line. Most of Ireland has a mid-green colour, which indicates the presence of rich pasture.

In the west, the lighter colour indicates moorland or bare rock and is also visible in the Cambrian Mountains in Wales, the Pennines and the Lake District in England, and the Scottish Highlands. Urban areas are shown as grey in colour.

Scale 1:4 000 000   1 cm on the map = 40 km on the ground

| 0 | 100km | 200km | 300km | 400km |

cm   cm

Height of the land (metres)

over 1000
400–1000
200–400
100–200
0–100
sea level
below sea level

	Highest mountains	
	Largest lakes	
	Longest rivers	
England		
Scafell Pike		978m
Windermere		15km²
Thames		346km
Severn		354km
Wales		
Snowdon		1085m
Bala Lake		5km²
Tywi		109km
Severn		354km
Scotland		
Ben Nevis		1344m
Loch Lomond		70km²
Tay		188km
Northern Ireland		
Slieve Donard		852m
Lough Neagh		396km²
Bann		128.7km
Ireland		
Carrauntoohill		1041m
Lough Corrib		176km²
Shannon		370km

Scale 1:4 600 000   1 cm on the map = 46 km on the ground

Height of the land (metres)	
Over 1000	
400 – 1000	
200 – 400	
Under 200	
sea level	

Key to map symbols

▲978   Height in metres

─────   International boundaries

LONDON ■ Over 1,000,000 inhabitants

Leeds ● 500,000 – 1,000,000 inhabitants

Plymouth ● 200,000 – 500,000 inhabitants

Oxford ● 100,000 – 200,000 inhabitants

Guildford ● 50,000 – 100,000 inhabitants

Dover · Under 50,000 inhabitants

ATLANTIC OCEAN

Celtic Sea

English Channel

North Sea

Irish Sea

SCOTLAND

NORTHERN IRELAND

IRELAND

WALES

ENGLAND

UNITED KINGDOM

FRANCE

COPYRIGHT PHILIP'S

COUNTRY FACTS

Country Name	Area (square kilometres)	Inhabitants (thousands 2015)	Capital City or Town
UNITED KINGDOM	**240,883**	**64,088**	**LONDON**
of which England	129,652	54,317	London
Wales	20,628	3,092	Cardiff
Scotland	77,097	5,348	Edinburgh
Northern Ireland	13,532	1,850	Belfast
*Isle of Man	572	88	Douglas
* Jersey	116	97	St. Helier
*Guernsey	63	66	St. Peter Port
IRELAND	**68,896**	**4,722**	**DUBLIN**

* Crown Dependencies which are not part of the U.K.

Scale 1:4 600 000

SCOTLAND
1. ABERDEEN CITY
2. DUNDEE CITY
3. WEST DUNBARTONSHIRE
4. EAST DUNBARTONSHIRE
5. CITY OF GLASGOW
6. INVERCLYDE
7. RENFREWSHIRE
8. EAST RENFREWSHIRE
9. NORTH LANARKSHIRE
10. FALKIRK
11. CLACKMANNANSHIRE
12. WEST LOTHIAN
13. CITY OF EDINBURGH
14. MIDLOTHIAN

WALES
15. SWANSEA
16. NEATH PORT TALBOT
17. BRIDGEND
18. RHONDDA CYNON TAFF
19. MERTHYR TYDFIL
20. CAERPHILLY
21. BLAENAU GWENT
22. TORFAEN
23. CARDIFF
24. NEWPORT

ENGLAND
25. HARTLEPOOL
26. DARLINGTON
27. STOCKTON-ON-TEES
28. MIDDLESBROUGH
29. REDCAR AND CLEVELAND
30. BLACKPOOL
31. BLACKBURN WITH DARWEN
32. HALTON
33. WARRINGTON
34. KINGSTON UPON HULL
35. NORTH EAST LINCOLNSHIRE
36. STOKE-ON-TRENT
37. TELFORD AND WREKIN
38. DERBY CITY
39. CITY OF NOTTINGHAM
40. LEICESTER CITY
41. RUTLAND
42. PETERBOROUGH
43. MILTON KEYNES
44. LUTON
45. NORTH SOMERSET
46. CITY OF BRISTOL
47. BATH AND N. E. SOMERSET
48. SWINDON
49. READING
50. WOKINGHAM
51. WINDSOR AND MAIDENHEAD
52. SLOUGH
53. BRACKNELL FOREST
54. THURROCK
55. SOUTHEND-ON-SEA
56. MEDWAY
57. PLYMOUTH
58. TORBAY
59. POOLE
60. BOURNEMOUTH
61. SOUTHAMPTON
62. PORTSMOUTH
63. BRIGHTON AND HOVE
64. BEDFORD
65. CENTRAL BEDFORDSHIRE

The map shows the 6 counties in Northern Ireland, the 32 unitary authorities in Wales and the 87 unitary authorities in England. Authorities which are too small to name on the map are numbered and listed separately.

Greater London and the 6 English metropolitan counties are coloured white on the map.

Greater London is divided into 32 borough councils and the City of London.

The 6 English metropolitan counties have 36 district councils.

● Capital cities

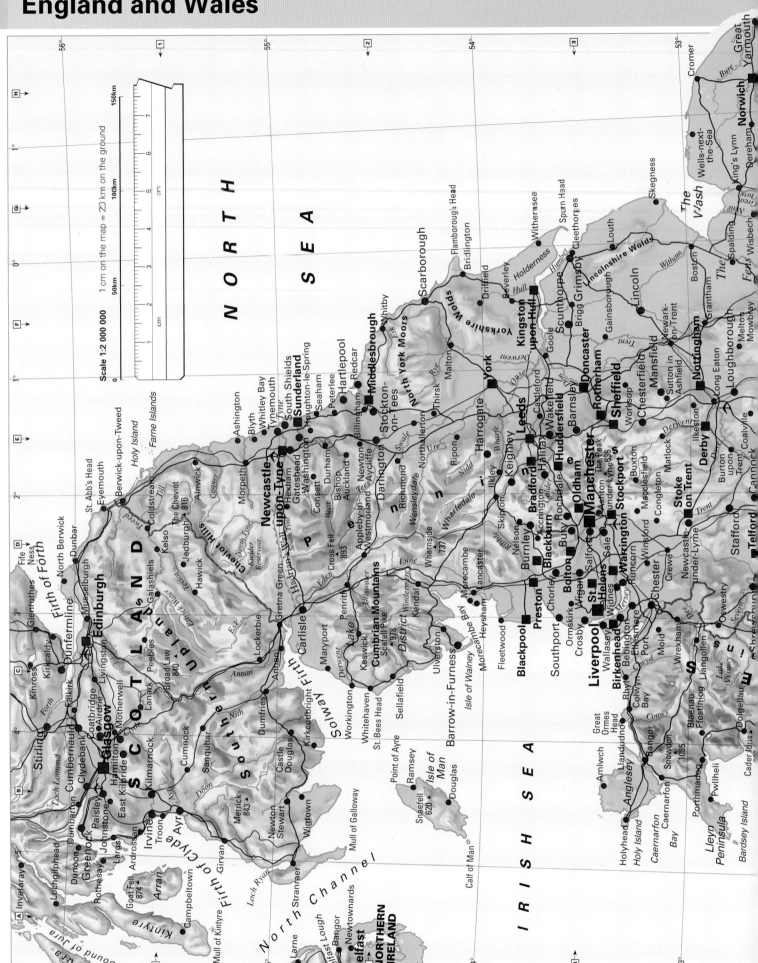

Scale 1:2 000 000

1 cm on the map = 20 km on the ground

0   50km   100km   150km

NORTH SEA

IRISH SEA

North Channel

Firth of Forth

SCOTLAND

Southern Uplands

NORTHERN IRELAND

Belfast

Newcastle-upon-Tyne

Sunderland

Middlesbrough

Hartlepool

Darlington

North York Moors

Scarborough

Leeds

Bradford

Manchester

Liverpool

Sheffield

Nottingham

Norwich

Yorkshire Wolds

Lincolnshire Wolds

The Wash

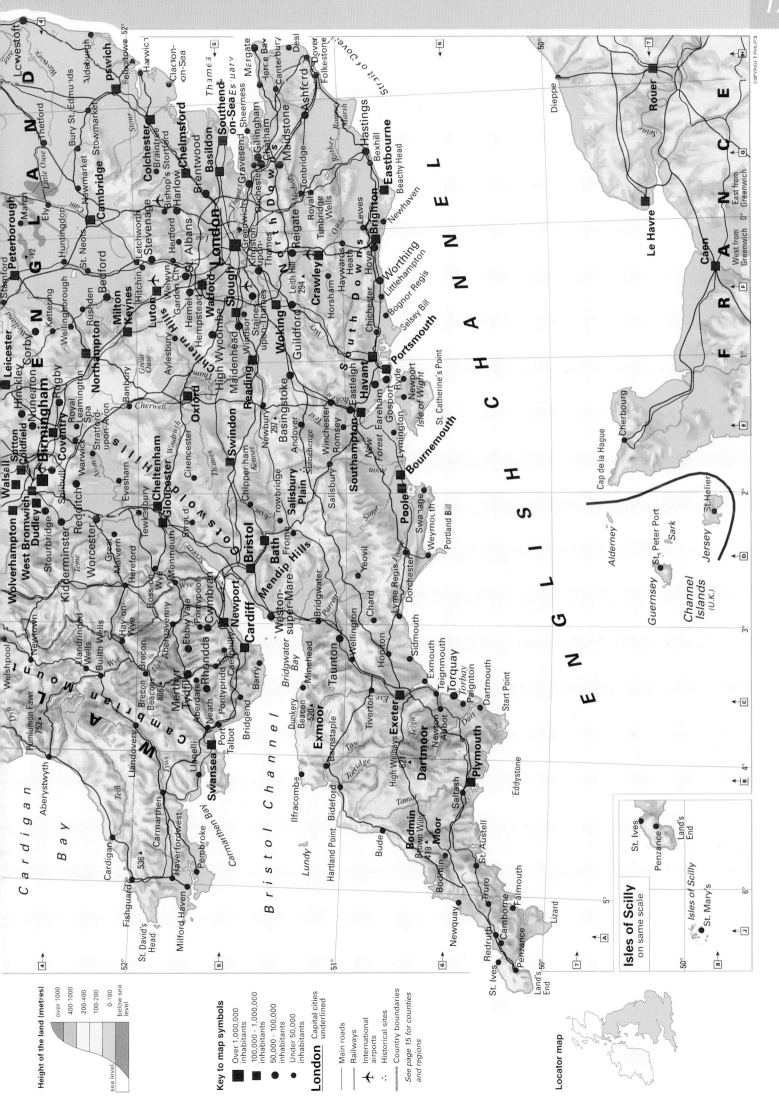

Height of the land (metres)

over 1000
400–1000
200–400
100–200
0–100
below sea level

sea level

Key to map symbols

● Over 1,000,000 inhabitants
■ 100,000 – 1,000,000 inhabitants
● 50,000 – 100,000 inhabitants
• Under 50,000 inhabitants

London Capital cities underlined

— Main roads
—— Railways
✈ International airports
∴ Historical sites
--- Country boundaries

See page 15 for counties and regions

Locator map

Isles of Scilly
on same scale

St. Ives
Penzance
Land's End

Isles of Scilly
St. Mary's

COPYRIGHT PHILIP'S

ENGLAND

FRANCE

ENGLISH CHANNEL

Cardigan Bay

Bristol Channel

Strait of Dover

Ipswich
Lowestoft
Felixstowe
Harwich
Aldeburgh
Thetford
Bury St. Edmunds
Stowmarket
Newmarket
Cambridge
Ely
Huntingdon
Peterborough
Stamford
March
Clacton-on-Sea
Colchester
Braintree
Bishop's Stortford
Harlow
Chelmsford
Brentwood
Basildon
Southend-on-Sea
Sheerness
Margate
Deal
Canterbury
Dover
Folkestone
Ashford
Maidstone
Chatham
Gillingham
Gravesend
Rochester
Hastings
Bexhill
Eastbourne
Beachy Head
Herne Bay
Royal Tunbridge Wells
Tonbridge
Sevenoaks
Reigate
Crawley
Haywards Heath
Lewes
Brighton
Hove
Worthing
Littlehampton
Bognor Regis
Selsey Bill
Chichester
Portsmouth
Havant
Gosport
Ryde
Newport
Isle of Wight
St. Catherine's Point
Lymington
Fareham
Eastleigh
Southampton
Winchester
Romsey
New Forest
Bournemouth
Poole
Swanage
Weymouth
Portland Bill
Dorchester
Lyme Regis
Sidmouth
Exmouth
Teignmouth
Dawlish
Torquay
Paignton
Torbay
Dartmouth
Start Point
Newton Abbot
Exeter
Tiverton
Taunton
Wellington
Honiton
Chard
Yeovil
Bridgwater
Minehead
Ilfracombe
Barnstaple
Bideford
Hartland Point
Bude
Newquay
St. Ives
St. Austell
Truro
Falmouth
Lizard
Redruth
Camborne
Penzance
Land's End
Eddystone
Saltash
Plymouth
Bodmin
Bodmin Moor
Brown Willy
Dartmoor
High Willhays

Thames
Stour
Little Ouse
Ouse
Cam
Great Ouse
Nene
Welland

Leicester
Hinckley
Nuneaton
Corby
Kettering
Rushden
Wellingborough
Rugby
Royal Leamington Spa
Warwick
Stratford-upon-Avon
Banbury
Bedford
St. Neots
Letchworth
Stevenage
Hitchin
Hertford
Welwyn Garden City
St. Albans
Hemel Hempstead
Watford
Luton
Milton Keynes
Northampton
Aylesbury
High Wycombe
Chiltern Hills
Maidenhead
Slough
London
Windsor
Staines-upon-Thames
Kingston-upon-Thames
Greenwich
Bromley
Woking
Guildford
Leith Hill 294
Horsham
Reading
Newbury
Basingstoke
Andover
Stonehenge
Salisbury
Salisbury Plain
Swindon
Cirencester
Gloucester
Cheltenham
Tewkesbury
Cotswold Hills
Oxford
Chipping Norton
Evesham
Worcester
Redditch
Bromsgrove
Birmingham
Coventry
Solihull
Dudley
West Bromwich
Sutton Coldfield
Walsall
Wolverhampton
Stourbridge
Kidderminster
Great Malvern
Hereford
Ross-on-Wye
Monmouth
Chepstow
Gloucester
Stroud
Cirencester
Chippenham
Trowbridge
Frome
Bath
Bristol
Weston-super-Mare
Mendip Hills
Bridgwater Bay
Dunkery Beacon 520
Exmoor

Trent
Avon
Severn
Wye
Teme
Cherwell
Windrush
Kennet
Thames
Test
Itchen
Arun
Adur
Ouse
Medway
Rother
Stour
Avon
Frome
Exe
Taw
Torridge
Teign
Dart
Tamar

WALES

Pwllheli
Newtown
Welshpool
Aberystwyth
Llandrindod Wells
Builth Wells
Llandovery
Brecon
Brecon Beacons 886
Merthyr Tydfil
Aberdare
Rhondda
Pontypridd
Caerphilly
Ebbw Vale
Abergavenny
Pontypool
Cwmbran
Newport
Cardiff
Barry
Bridgend
Port Talbot
Neath
Swansea
Llanelli
Carmarthen
Haverfordwest
Milford Haven
Pembroke
Fishguard
St. David's Head
Cardigan
Plynlimon Fawr 752

Cambrian Mountains

Dyfi
Teifi
Tywi
Towy
Usk

Channel Islands (U.K.)
Alderney
Cap de la Hague
Cherbourg
Guernsey
St. Peter Port
Sark
Jersey
St. Helier

Le Havre
Rouen
Caen
Dieppe
Seine

West from Greenwich 0° East from Greenwich

Orkney Islands
on same scale

Shetland Islands
on same scale

Locator map

Scale 1:2 000 000   1 cm on the map = 20 km on the ground

0   50km   100km   150km   200km

ATLANTIC

OCEAN

SCOTLAND
Campbeltown
Mull of Kintyre
Loch Ryan
Stranraer

Arran

North Channel

Malin Head
Tory Island
Inishowen Peninsula
Giants Causeway
Rathlin Island
Bloody Foreland
Buncrana
Moville
Colcraine
Ballycastle
Errigal 752
Lough Swilly
Ballymoney
Trostan 554
Mountains of Antrim
Larne
Arranmore
Letterkenny
Derry/Londonderry
Ballymena
Antrim
Carrickfergus
Belfast Lough
Bangor
Rossan Point
Strabane
Sperrin Mountains
Sawel 683
Mourne
Derg
676
Newtownabbey
Belfast
Newtownards
Donegal
Omagh
Cookstown
NORTHERN
Lisburn
Lagan
Ards Peninsula
Killybegs
Dungannon
Lough Neagh
Donegal Bay
Bundoran
Ballyshannon
IRELAND
Portadown
Lurgan
Ballyquintin Point
Lower Lough Erne
Armagh
Banbridge
Downpatrick
Erris Head
Killala Bay
Sligo Bay
Enniskillen
Erne
Monaghan
Newry
Slieve Donard 852
Dundrum Bay
Mullet Peninsula
Sligo
Upper Lough Erne
Finn
Mourne Mountains
Warrenpoint
Ballina
Colooney
Shannon
Belturbet
Annalee
Cootehill
Dundalk
Louth
Lough Conn 722
Lough Allen
Cavan
Carrickmacross
Dundalk Bay
Achill Island
Castlebar
Charlestown
Boyle
Carrick-on-Shannon
Clew Bay
Knock
Longford
Navan
Drogheda
IRISH
Clare Island
Westport
Claremorris
Castlerea
Blackwater
Balbriggan
Inishturk
Mweelrea 819
Lough Mask
Ballinrobe
Roscommon
Lough Ree
Mullingar
Boyne
Swords
Malahide
SEA
Inishbofin
Rode
Inny
Ireland's Eye
Clifden 730
Tuam
Lough Corrib
Leinster
Maynooth
Howth Head
Connemara
Clare
Athlone
Edenderry
Dublin
Slyne Head
CONNAUGHT
Galway
Ballinasloe
Liffey
Dun Laoghaire
Inishmore
Galway Bay
Loughrea
Shannon
Tullamore
Bog of Allen
Naas
Newbridge
Bray
Greystones
Aran Islands
Gort
Birr
IRELAND
Portlaoise
Kildare
Poulaphouca Reservoir
Wicklow Mountains
Cliffs of Moher
Lough Derg
Roscrea
Athy
Lugnaquillia 926
Wicklow
Ennis
Killaloe
Nenagh
Portarlington
Carlow
Tullow
Mizen Head
Milltown Malbay
Keeper Hill 694
Thurles
Nore
Kilkenny
Mount Leinster 796
Arklow
Kilkee
Kilrush
Limerick
Suir
Cashel
Barrow
Enniscorthy
Gorey
Loop Head
Mouth of the Shannon
Listowel
Newcastle West
Tipperary
Caher
Carrick-on-Suir
New Ross
Wexford
Kerry Head
Tralee Bay
Munster
Galtymore 920
Clonmel
Waterford
Rosslare Harbour
Brandon Mountain 953
Tralee
Mitchelstown
Knockmealdown Mountains
792
Carnsore Point
Dingle Peninsula
Maine
Kanturk
Fermoy
Blackwater
Tramore
Hook Head
Saltee Islands
Dingle
Slea Head
Dingle Bay
Killarney
Mallow
Dungarvan
St. David's Head
Macgillycuddy's Reeks 1041
Carrauntoohill
696
Boggeragh Mountains
Blarney
Youghal
WALES
Valencia Island
Cahirciveen
Kenmare
Lee
Cork
Iveragh Peninsula
Kenmare
Caha Mountains
Passage West
Cobh
Carrigaline
Castletown Bearhaven
Bantry
Bandon
Kinsale
Crow Head
Bear Island
Bantry Bay
Clonakilty
Old Head of Kinsale
St. George's Channel
Clear Island
Skibbereen
Fastnet Rock
Cape Clear

CELTIC SEA

West from Greenwich

COPYRIGHT PHILIP'S

Height of the land (metres)

over 1000
400–1000
200–400
100–200
0–100
sea level
below sea level

Key to map symbols

■ Over 1,000,000 inhabitants
■ 100,000 – 1,000,000 inhabitants
● 50,000 – 100,000 inhabitants
• Under 50,000 inhabitants

Dublin Capital cities underlined

Scale 1:2 000 000

— Main roads
— Railways
✈ International airports
---- Country boundaries

See page 15 for counties and regions

Locator map

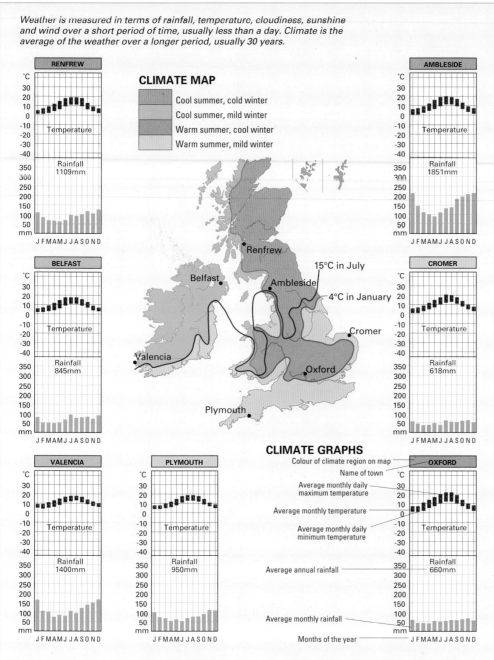

Weather is measured in terms of rainfall, temperature, cloudiness, sunshine and wind over a short period of time, usually less than a day. Climate is the average of the weather over a longer period, usually 30 years.

RENFREW

AMBLESIDE

CLIMATE MAP

Cool summer, cold winter
Cool summer, mild winter
Warm summer, cool winter
Warm summer, mild winter

BELFAST

15°C in July

4°C in January

CROMER

VALENCIA

PLYMOUTH

CLIMATE GRAPHS

Colour of climate region on map
Name of town
Average monthly daily maximum temperature
Average monthly temperature
Average monthly daily minimum temperature
Average annual rainfall
Average monthly rainfall
Months of the year

OXFORD

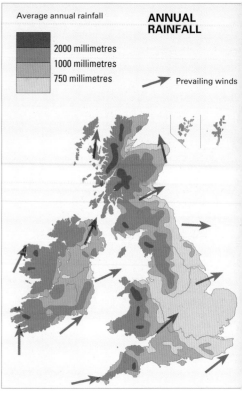

ANNUAL RAINFALL

Average annual rainfall

2000 millimetres
1000 millimetres
750 millimetres

Prevailing winds

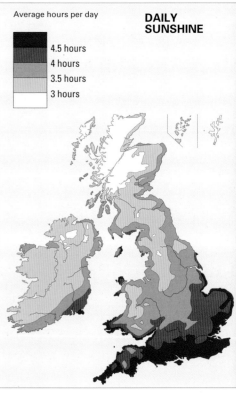

DAILY SUNSHINE

Average hours per day

4.5 hours
4 hours
3.5 hours
3 hours

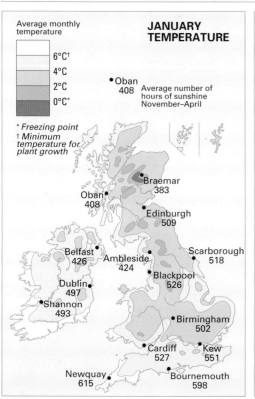

JANUARY TEMPERATURE

Average monthly temperature

6°C†
4°C
2°C
0°C*

* Freezing point
† Minimum temperature for plant growth

Oban 408 — Average number of hours of sunshine November–April

Braemar 383
Oban 408
Edinburgh 509
Scarborough 518
Belfast 426
Ambleside 424
Blackpool 526
Dublin 497
Shannon 493
Birmingham 502
Cardiff 527
Kew 551
Newquay 615
Bournemouth 598

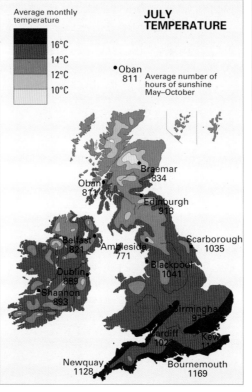

JULY TEMPERATURE

Average monthly temperature

16°C
14°C
12°C
10°C

Oban 811 — Average number of hours of sunshine May–October

Braemar 834
Oban 811
Edinburgh 918
Scarborough 1035
Belfast 821
Ambleside 771
Blackpool 1041
Dublin 889
Shannon 893
Birmingham 977
Cardiff 102
Kew 11
Newquay 1128
Bournemouth 1169

Temperature Records
Highest
38.5°C Brogdale near Faversham, (Kent) 10 August 2003
Lowest
-27.2°C Braemar, Aberdeenshire, 10 January 1982 and 11 February 1895, Altnaharra, Highland, 30 December 1995

Rainfall Records
Highest 24 hour total
279 mm Martinstown, near Dorchester, Dorset, 18 July 1955
The highest total for any 24 hour period is 316mm at Seathwaite, Cumbria on 19 November 2009.

Sunshine Records
Highest monthly total
390 hours Eastbourne and Hastings, Sussex, July 1911
Lowest monthly total
0 hours Westminster, Greater London, December 1890

Winds (highest gusts)
150 knots Cairngorm, 20 March 1986

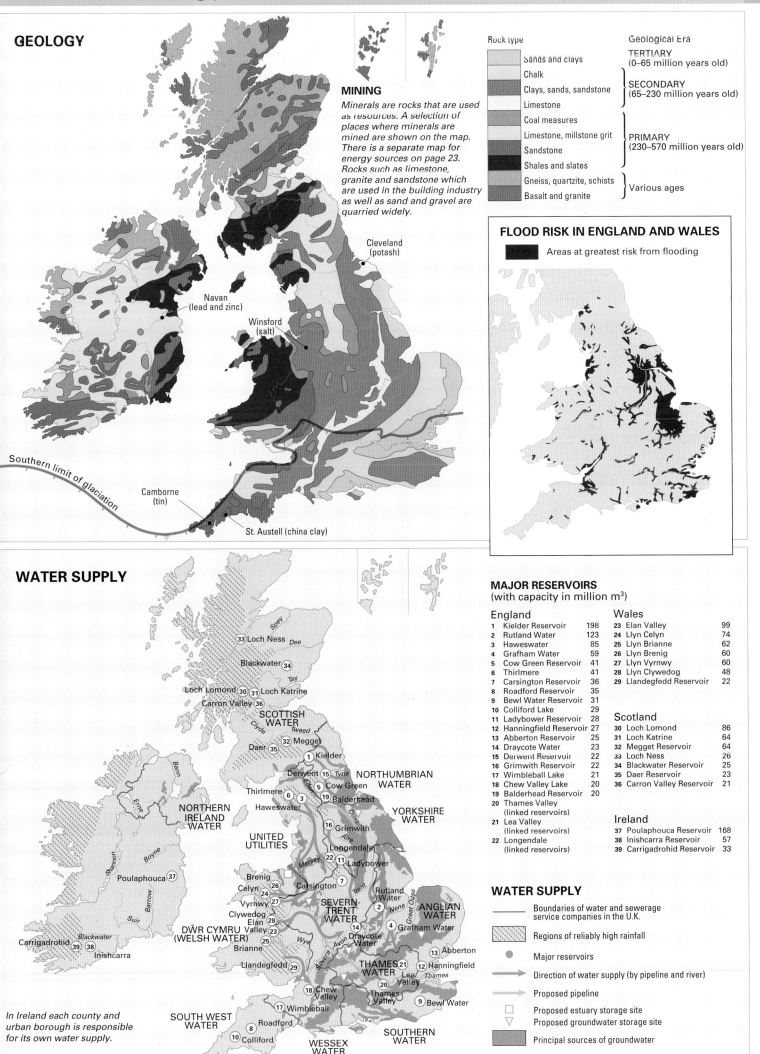

GEOLOGY

Rock type	Geological Era
Sands and clays	TERTIARY (0–65 million years old)
Chalk	SECONDARY (65–230 million years old)
Clays, sands, sandstone	
Limestone	
Coal measures	PRIMARY (230–570 million years old)
Limestone, millstone grit	
Sandstone	
Shales and slates	
Gneiss, quartzite, schists	Various ages
Basalt and granite	

MINING

Minerals are rocks that are used as resources. A selection of places where minerals are mined are shown on the map. There is a separate map for energy sources on page 23. Rocks such as limestone, granite and sandstone which are used in the building industry as well as sand and gravel are quarried widely.

Cleveland (potash)

Navan (lead and zinc)

Winsford (salt)

Southern limit of glaciation

Camborne (tin)

St. Austell (china clay)

FLOOD RISK IN ENGLAND AND WALES

■ Areas at greatest risk from flooding

WATER SUPPLY

In Ireland each county and urban borough is responsible for its own water supply.

Spey
Dee
33 Loch Ness
Blackwater 34
Tay
Loch Lomond 30 31 Loch Katrine
Carron Valley 36
SCOTTISH WATER
Clyde
Tweed
32 Megget
Daer 35
1 Kielder
Derwent 15 Tyne
5 Cow Green
NORTHUMBRIAN WATER
Thirlmere 6 3 19 Balderhead
NORTHERN IRELAND WATER
Haweswater
YORKSHIRE WATER
Ouse
16 Grimwith
Aire
UNITED UTILITIES
Mersey
22 11 Ladybower
Longendale
Brenig 26
Celyn 24
Carsington 7
Trent
Rutland Water
SEVERN-TRENT WATER
Vyrnwy 27
Clywedog 28
Elan Valley 23
2 Nene
Great Ouse
ANGLIAN WATER
DWR CYMRU (WELSH WATER)
Brianne 25
14
4 Grafham Water
Wye
Severn
Avon
Draycote Water
13 Abberton
Llandegfedd 29
THAMES WATER 21
Lea Valley
12 Hanningfield
Thames
18 Chew Valley
20 Thames Valley
9 Bewl Water
17 Wimbleball
SOUTH WEST WATER
Roadford
SOUTHERN WATER
8
10 Colliford
WESSEX WATER

Bann
Erne
Shannon
Boyne
Poulaphouca 37
Barrow
Suir
Carrigadrohid 39 38
Inishcarra
Blackwater

MAJOR RESERVOIRS
(with capacity in million m³)

England
1	Kielder Reservoir	198
2	Rutland Water	123
3	Haweswater	85
4	Grafham Water	59
5	Cow Green Reservoir	41
6	Thirlmere	41
7	Carsington Reservoir	36
8	Roadford Reservoir	35
9	Bewl Water Reservoir	31
10	Colliford Lake	29
11	Ladybower Reservoir	28
12	Hanningfield Reservoir	27
13	Abberton Reservoir	25
14	Draycote Water	23
15	Derwent Reservoir	22
16	Grimwith Reservoir	22
17	Wimbleball Lake	21
18	Chew Valley Lake	20
19	Balderhead Reservoir	20
20	Thames Valley (linked reservoirs)	
21	Lea Valley (linked reservoirs)	
22	Longendale (linked reservoirs)	

Wales
23	Elan Valley	99
24	Llyn Celyn	74
25	Llyn Brianne	62
26	Llyn Brenig	60
27	Llyn Vyrnwy	60
28	Llyn Clywedog	48
29	Llandegfedd Reservoir	22

Scotland
30	Loch Lomond	86
31	Loch Katrine	64
32	Megget Reservoir	64
33	Loch Ness	26
34	Blackwater Reservoir	25
35	Daer Reservoir	23
36	Carron Valley Reservoir	21

Ireland
37	Poulaphouca Reservoir	168
38	Inishcarra Reservoir	57
39	Carrigadrohid Reservoir	33

WATER SUPPLY

——— Boundaries of water and sewerage service companies in the U.K.

▨ Regions of reliably high rainfall

● Major reservoirs

→ Direction of water supply (by pipeline and river)

→ Proposed pipeline

□ Proposed estuary storage site

▽ Proposed groundwater storage site

▨ Principal sources of groundwater

COPYRIGHT PHILIP'S

TYPES OF FARM

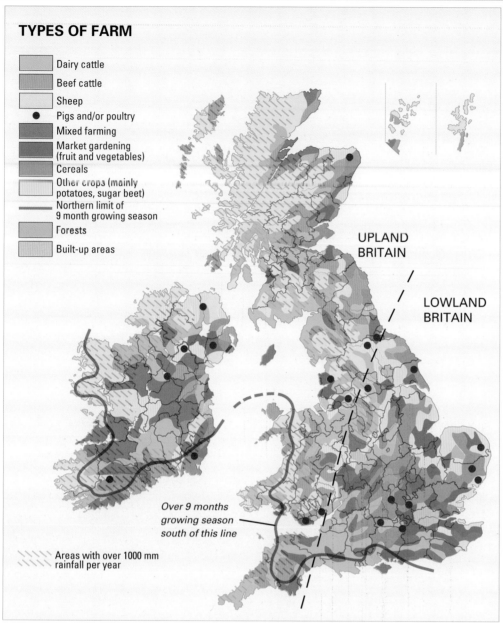

- Dairy cattle
- Beef cattle
- Sheep
- Pigs and/or poultry
- Mixed farming
- Market gardening (fruit and vegetables)
- Cereals
- Other crops (mainly potatoes, sugar beet)
- Northern limit of 9 month growing season
- Forests
- Built-up areas

UPLAND BRITAIN

LOWLAND BRITAIN

Over 9 months growing season south of this line

Areas with over 1000 mm rainfall per year

CEREAL FARMING

The percentage of the total farmland used for growing cereals in 2013

- Over 40%
- 25 – 40%
- 10 – 25%
- 5 – 10%
- 0 – 5%

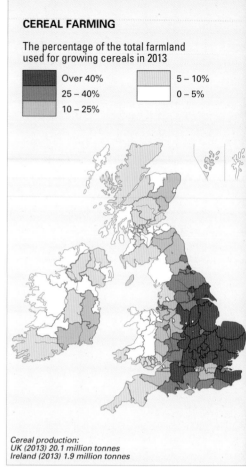

Cereal production:
UK (2013) 20.1 million tonnes
Ireland (2013) 1.9 million tonnes

DAIRY FARMING

The number of dairy cows per 100 hectares of farmland

- Over 40
- 30 – 40
- 20 – 30
- 10 – 20
- 0 – 10

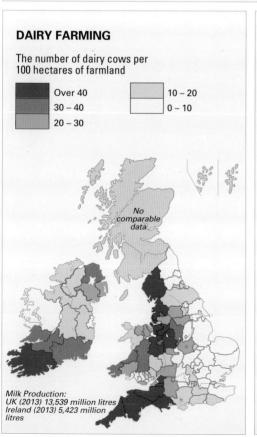

No comparable data

Milk Production:
UK (2013) 13,539 million litres
Ireland (2013) 5,423 million litres

COPYRIGHT PHILIP'S

LIVESTOCK FARMING

The number of beef cattle, sheep and pigs per 100 hectares of farmland

- Over 400
- 300 – 400
- 200 – 300
- 100 – 200
- Under 100

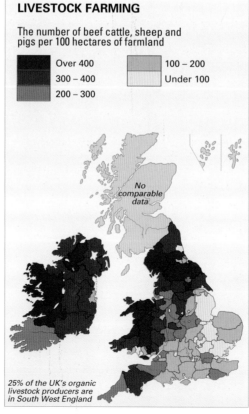

No comparable data

25% of the UK's organic livestock producers are in South West England

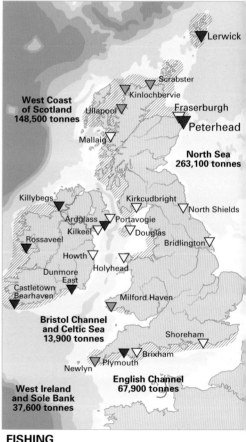

Lerwick
Scrabster
Kinlochbervie
West Coast of Scotland 148,500 tonnes
Ullapool
Fraserburgh
Peterhead
Mallaig
North Sea 263,100 tonnes
Killybegs
Kirkcudbright
North Shields
Ardglass
Portavogie
Kilkeel
Douglas
Rossaveel
Bridlington
Howth
Holyhead
Dunmore East
Castletown Bearhaven
Milford Haven
Bristol Channel and Celtic Sea 13,900 tonnes
Shoreham
Brixham
Plymouth
Newlyn
English Channel 67,900 tonnes
West Ireland and Sole Bank 37,600 tonnes

FISHING

Major fishing ports by size of catch landed

- ▽ Mainly deep sea fish (e.g. cod)
- ▼ Mainly shallow sea fish (e.g. mackerel)
- ▽ Mainly shellfish e.g. lobster

The most important inshore fishing ground

North Sea 263,100 tonnes

Total amount caught in each fishing region 2012

1000 500 200 100 50 m   Depth of sea in metres

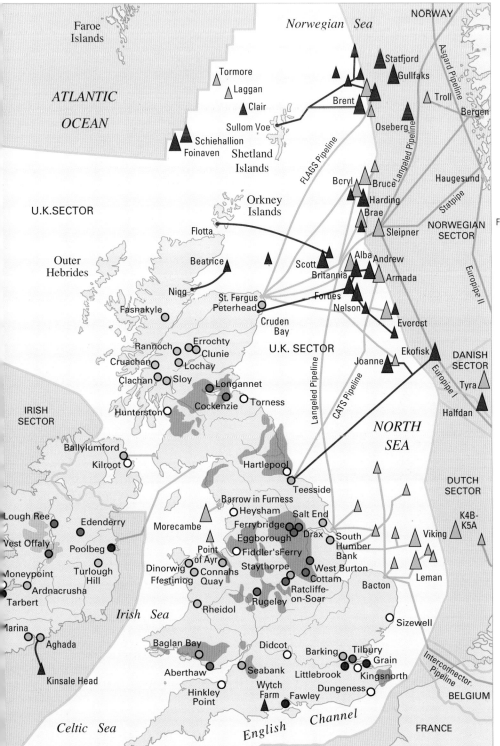

ENERGY CONSUMPTION BY FUEL

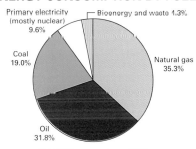

- Primary electricity (mostly nuclear) 9.6%
- Bioenergy and waste 4.3%
- Coal 19.0%
- Oil 31.8%
- Natural gas 35.3%

Total U.K. consumption in 2013: 205.9 million tonnes of oil equivalent

CHANGES IN ELECTRICITY GENERATION

Fuel used in the generation of electricity in the U.K. 1980 – 2010 (2013 percentages are in brackets)

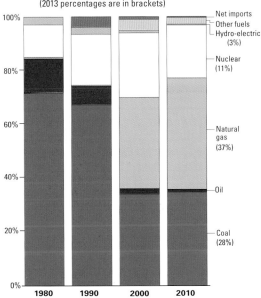

- Net imports
- Other fuels
- Hydro-electric (3%)
- Nuclear (11%)
- Natural gas (37%)
- Oil
- Coal (28%)

RENEWABLE ENERGY

The amount of energy generated from renewable sources in kilowatt hours

- 30,000
- 20,000
- 10,000
- 5,000
- Major wind farm
- Possible sites for tidal power generation

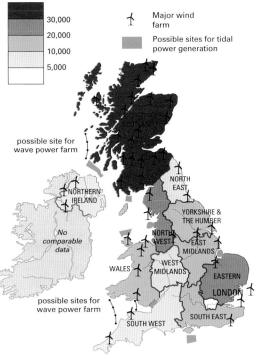

possible site for wave power farm

possible sites for wave power farm

No comparable data

ENERGY SOURCES

- Coalfield
- Coal-fired power station
- Peat-cutting area in Ireland
- Peat-fired power station
- Oilfield
- Oil pipeline (with terminal)
- Oil-fired power station
- Gasfield
- Gas pipeline (with terminal)
- Gas-fired power station
- Coal, biomass & gas-fired power station
- Hydro-electric power station
- Nuclear power station

Only major power stations and fields are shown

- International dividing line

ENERGY IMPORTS

COAL IMPORTS

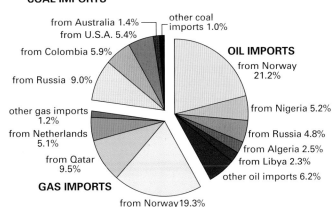

- from Australia 1.4%
- from U.S.A. 5.4%
- other coal imports 1.0%
- from Colombia 5.9%
- from Russia 9.0%
- other gas imports 1.2%
- from Netherlands 5.1%
- from Qatar 9.5%

GAS IMPORTS

- from Norway 19.3%

OIL IMPORTS

- from Norway 21.2%
- from Nigeria 5.2%
- from Russia 4.8%
- from Algeria 2.5%
- from Libya 2.3%
- other oil imports 6.2%

Total U.K. imports 2012 130.9 million tonnes of oil equivalent

CHANGES TO COAL MINING IN THE U.K.

	1960	1980	2010
Production (million tonnes)	195	126	18
Number of employees (thousands)	631	297	9
Number of deep mines	698	211	12

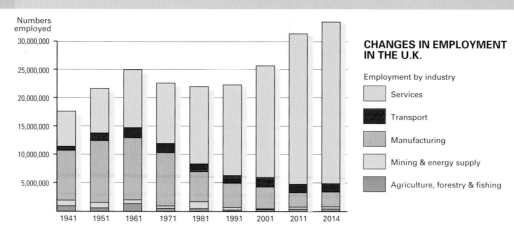

CHANGES IN EMPLOYMENT IN THE U.K.

Employment by industry

- Services
- Transport
- Manufacturing
- Mining & energy supply
- Agriculture, forestry & fishing

▲ Canary Wharf, London, is a centre of banking – an important part of the service industry.

▲ These Mini Clubman cars are being manufactured at the BMW factory, Oxford.

▲ An engineer is shown working on a jet engine in the Rolls-Royce factory, Derby.

INCOME

The average gross weekly earnings of males and females in full employment in 2012

- Over £600
- £550 – £600
- £500 – £550
- £475 – £500
- Under £475

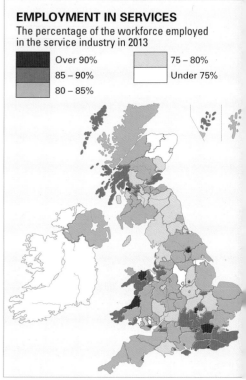

Average weekly earnings (2012)
U.K. £513
Ireland €692

EMPLOYMENT IN SERVICES

The percentage of the workforce employed in the service industry in 2013

- Over 90%
- 85 – 90%
- 80 – 85%
- 75 – 80%
- Under 75%

EMPLOYMENT IN MANUFACTURING INDUSTRY

The percentage of the workforce employed in manufacturing in 2013

- Over 15%
- 12.5 – 15%
- 10 – 12.5%
- 7.5 – 10%
- 5 – 7.5%
- Under 5%

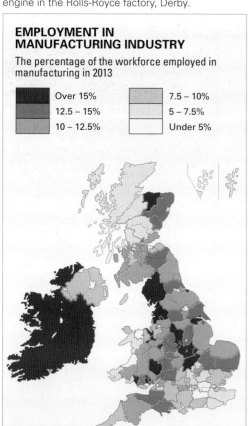

UNEMPLOYMENT

The percentage of the workforce unemployed in 2013

- Over 10%
- 8 – 10%
- 6 – 8%
- Under 6%

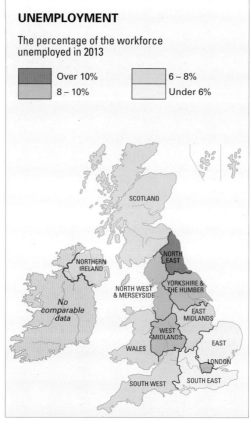

U.K. TRADE

Trade is balanced by money coming in for services such as banking and insurance.

Total Imports 2013
£368.0 billion

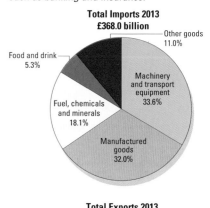

- Machinery and transport equipment 33.6%
- Manufactured goods 32.0%
- Fuel, chemicals and minerals 18.1%
- Other goods 11.0%
- Food and drink 5.3%

Total Exports 2013
£282.2 billion

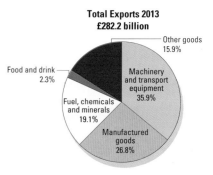

- Machinery and transport equipment 35.9%
- Manufactured goods 26.8%
- Fuel, chemicals and minerals 19.1%
- Other goods 15.9%
- Food and drink 2.3%

POPULATION FACTS

U.K. Population 2015	64,088,000
of which England	54,317,000
Scotland	5,348,000
Wales	3,092,000
Northern Ireland	1,331,000
Ireland Population 2015	**4,892,000**

AGE STRUCTURE OF THE U.K. IN 1901 AND 2014

The age structure shows how old people are and the percentage in each age group that is male and female. Each diagram is called a population pyramid. For example, in 1901, 20% of the female population was aged between 10–19. In 2014, about 11% were in this group.

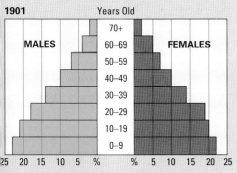

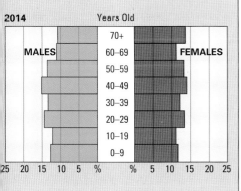

POPULATION DENSITY

Number of people per square kilometre in 2014

- Over 1000
- 500 – 1000
- 200 – 500
- 100 – 200
- 50 – 100
- 25 – 50
- Under 25

The average density for the U.K. is 265 people per km².

The average density for Ireland is 70 people per km².

Population of major cities

- Over 5,000,000
- 1,000,000 – 5,000,000
- 400,000 – 1,000,000
- 200,000 – 400,000
- 100,000 – 200,000

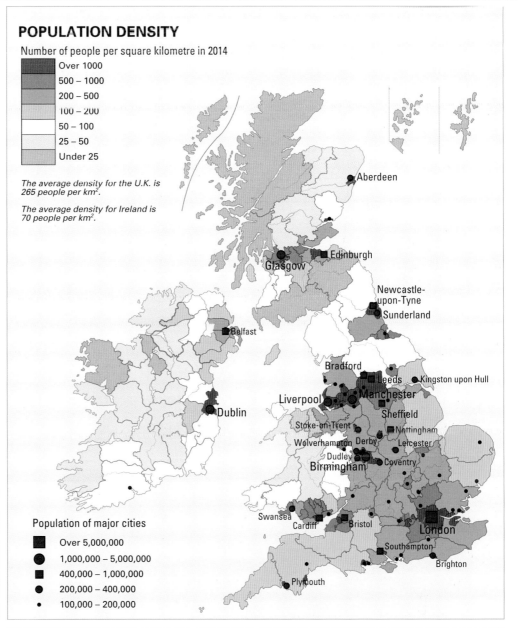

NATIONALITY

Non-British as a percentage of total population in 2013

- Over 20%
- 10 – 20%
- 5 – 10%
- 0 – 5%

360 000 Total number of non-British people in each region

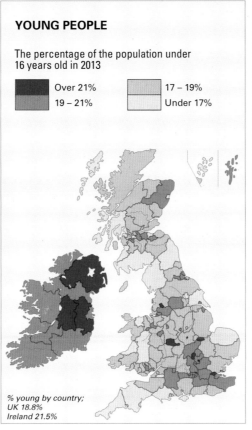

% foreign born by country; UK 7.8% Ireland 13.1%

YOUNG PEOPLE

The percentage of the population under 16 years old in 2013

- Over 21%
- 19 – 21%
- 17 – 19%
- Under 17%

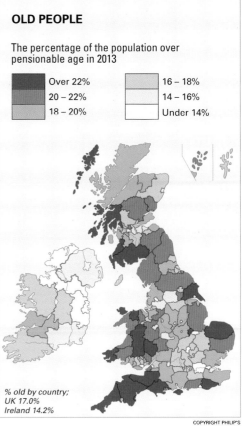

% young by country; UK 18.8% Ireland 21.5%

OLD PEOPLE

The percentage of the population over pensionable age in 2013

- Over 22%
- 20 – 22%
- 18 – 20%
- 16 – 18%
- 14 – 16%
- Under 14%

% old by country; UK 17.0% Ireland 14.2%

COPYRIGHT PHILIP'S

ROADS AND FERRIES

- M6 Motorways
- Other main roads
- Principal car ferry routes

RAILWAYS

- Electrified lines
- Other main lines
- High-speed rail link
- Planned high-speed rail link (HS2)

The fastest journey time from London to Paris via the Channel Tunnel is now 2 hours 15 minutes, London to Brussels is 1 hour 51 minutes.

AIRPORTS

Passenger traffic in millions (2013)

70,000
35,000
10,000
5,000
1,000

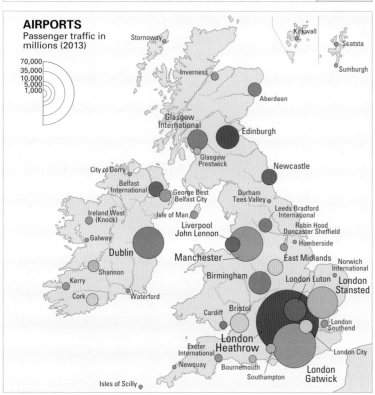

SEAPORTS

Goods traffic by port in million tonnes (2012)

60,000
30,000
10,000
5,000

TOURIST TRAFFIC

Millions of visitors from U.K. (2013)

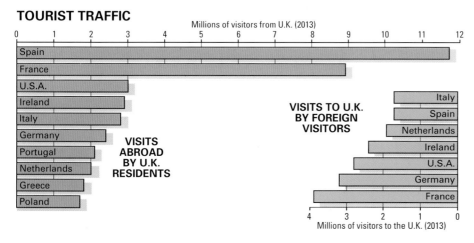

VISITS ABROAD BY U.K. RESIDENTS

Spain, France, U.S.A., Ireland, Italy, Germany, Portugal, Netherlands, Greece, Poland

VISITS TO U.K. BY FOREIGN VISITORS

Italy, Spain, Netherlands, Ireland, U.S.A., Germany, France

Millions of visitors to the U.K. (2013)

▲ **Eurostar at St. Pancras International.** This station is the London terminus of the high-speed rail link to Europe, High Speed 1.

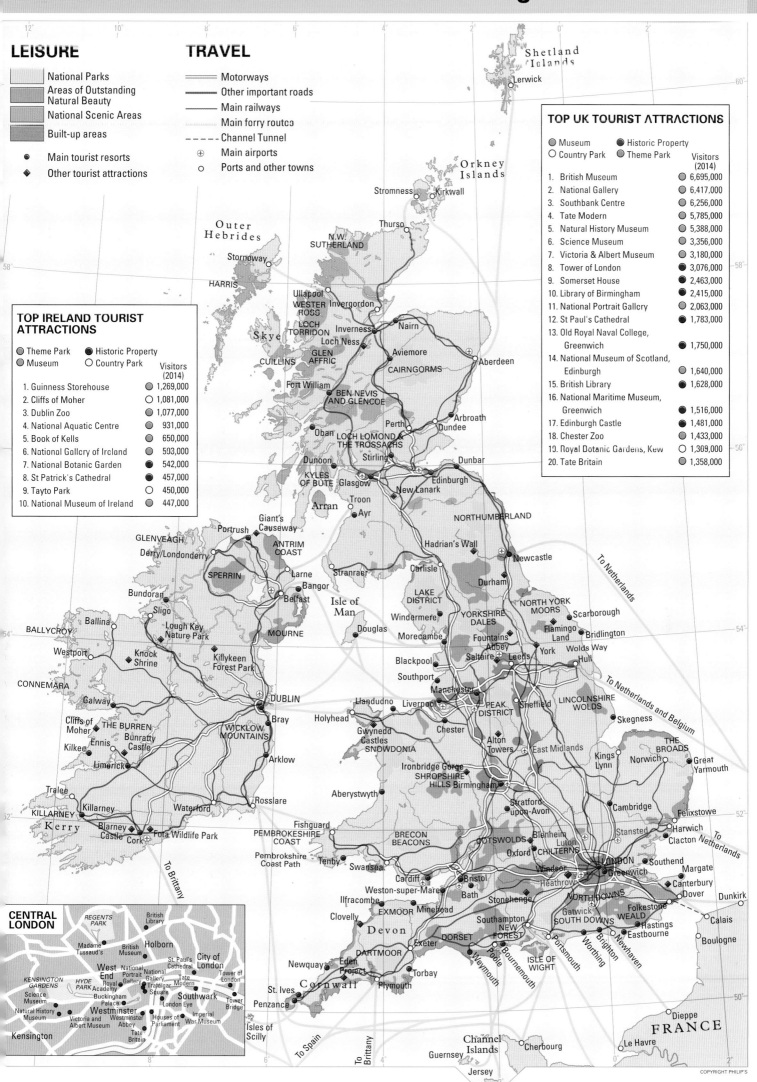

LEISURE

- National Parks
- Areas of Outstanding Natural Beauty
- National Scenic Areas
- Built-up areas
- Main tourist resorts
- Other tourist attractions

TRAVEL

- Motorways
- Other important roads
- Main railways
- Main ferry routes
- Channel Tunnel
- Main airports
- Ports and other towns

TOP UK TOURIST ATTRACTIONS

- Museum
- Country Park
- Historic Property
- Theme Park

		Visitors (2014)
1.	British Museum	6,695,000
2.	National Gallery	6,417,000
3.	Southbank Centre	6,256,000
4.	Tate Modern	5,785,000
5.	Natural History Museum	5,388,000
6.	Science Museum	3,356,000
7.	Victoria & Albert Museum	3,180,000
8.	Tower of London	3,076,000
9.	Somerset House	2,463,000
10.	Library of Birmingham	2,415,000
11.	National Portrait Gallery	2,063,000
12.	St Paul's Cathedral	1,783,000
13.	Old Royal Naval College, Greenwich	1,750,000
14.	National Museum of Scotland, Edinburgh	1,640,000
15.	British Library	1,628,000
16.	National Maritime Museum, Greenwich	1,516,000
17.	Edinburgh Castle	1,481,000
18.	Chester Zoo	1,433,000
19.	Royal Botanic Gardens, Kew	1,309,000
20.	Tate Britain	1,358,000

TOP IRELAND TOURIST ATTRACTIONS

- Theme Park
- Museum
- Historic Property
- Country Park

		Visitors (2014)
1.	Guinness Storehouse	1,269,000
2.	Cliffs of Moher	1,081,000
3.	Dublin Zoo	1,077,000
4.	National Aquatic Centre	931,000
5.	Book of Kells	650,000
6.	National Gallery of Ireland	593,000
7.	National Botanic Garden	542,000
8.	St Patrick's Cathedral	457,000
9.	Tayto Park	450,000
10.	National Museum of Ireland	447,000

CENTRAL LONDON

REGENTS PARK
British Library
Madame Tussaud's
British Museum
Holborn
St. Paul's Cathedral
City of London
West End
National Portrait Gallery
National Gallery
Tate Modern
Tower of London
KENSINGTON GARDENS
HYDE PARK
Royal Academy
Trafalgar Square
Southwark
Tower Bridge
Science Museum
Buckingham Palace
Natural History Museum
Victoria and Albert Museum
Westminster
Westminster Abbey
Houses of Parliament
Imperial War Museum
Kensington
Tate Britain
London Eye

COPYRIGHT PHILIP'S

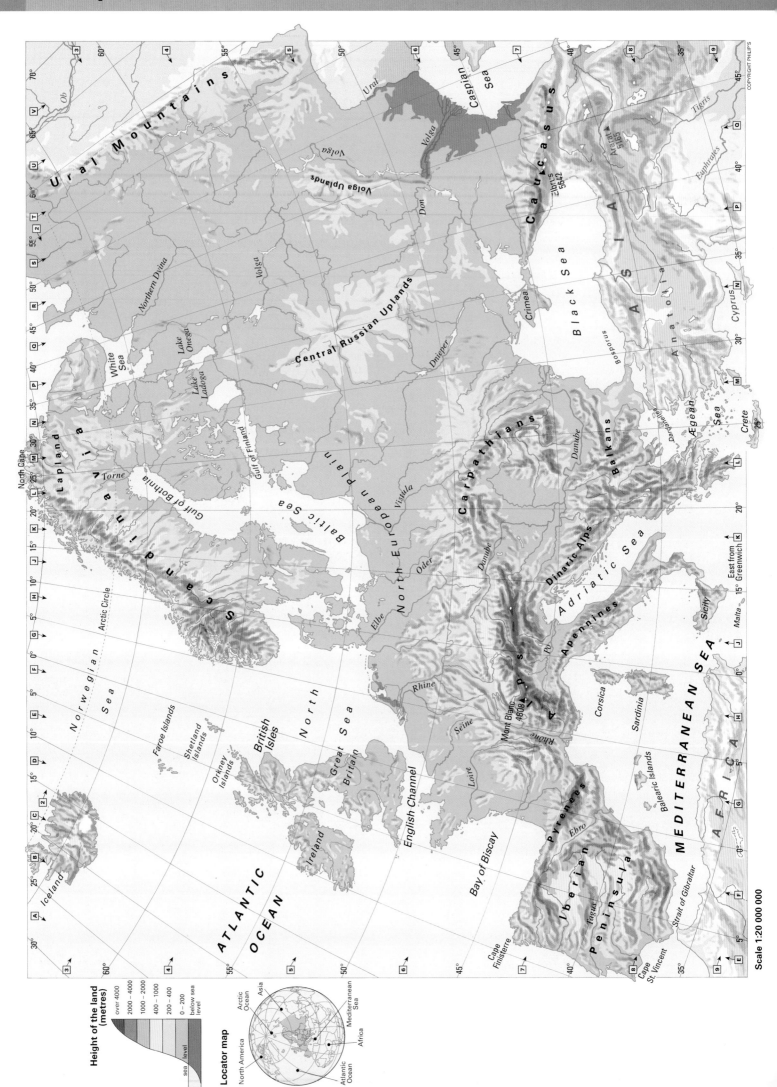

Height of the land
(metres)

over 4000
2000 – 4000
1000 – 2000
400 – 1000
200 – 400
0 – 200
below sea
level

sea level

Locator map

North America
Arctic Ocean
Asia
Mediterranean Sea
Africa
Atlantic Ocean

Scale 1:20 000 000

COPYRIGHT PHILIP'S

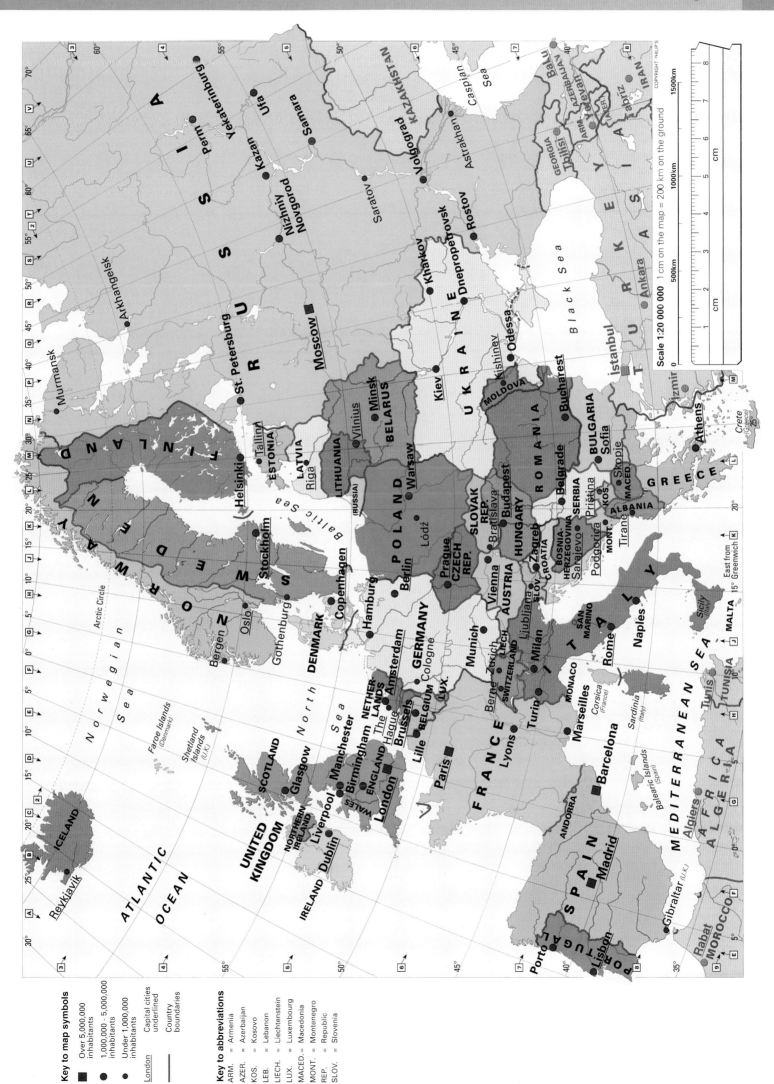

Main map (European Union)

ICELAND

ATLANTIC OCEAN

NORWAY

FINLAND €

SWEDEN

ESTONIA €

LATVIA

LITHUANIA
(RUSSIA) €

IRELAND €

UNITED KINGDOM

DENMARK

NETHERLANDS

Brussels
BELGIUM €
LUXEMBOURG €
Luxembourg
Strasbourg

GERMANY €

POLAND

BELARUS

RUSSIA

UKRAINE

CZECH REPUBLIC

SLOVAK REPUBLIC

MOLDOVA

FRANCE €

LIECHTENSTEIN
AUSTRIA €
SWITZERLAND

HUNGARY

ROMANIA

GEORGIA

AZERBAIJAN

ARMENIA

Caspian Sea

PORTUGAL €

SPAIN €

ANDORRA

MONACO

SAN MARINO

SLOVENIA €
CROATIA
BOSNIA HERZ.
SERBIA

Black Sea

VATICAN CITY

ITALY €

MONTENEGRO
KOSOVO
MACEDONIA

BULGARIA €

TURKEY

Ceuta (Sp.)
Gibraltar (U.K.)
Melilla (Sp.)

Mediterranean Sea

Africa

MALTA €

GREECE €

Asia

CYPRUS €

EUROPEAN UNION

This map shows the members of the European Union and the year that they joined.

- Founder member (Treaty of Rome 195
- Joined in 1973
- Joined in 1981
- Joined in 1986
- Joined in 1990 (German unification
- Joined in 1995
- Joined in 2004
- Joined in 2007
- Joined in 2013

○ HQ of European institutions

€ Euro-zone

Non-members

Albania, Macedonia, Montenegro, Serbia and Turkey have applied for membership of the EU

WEALTH map

Norwegian Fjords
Saimaa
St. Petersburg
Stockholm
Moscow
Edinburgh
Dublin
Copenhagen
Öland
Amsterdam
London
Berlin
Brussels
Prague
Tatra
Brittany
Paris
Disneyland Paris
Vienna
Budapest
Crimea
Alps
Lourdes
Venice
Adriatic Coast
Black Sea Coast
Lisbon
Pyrenees
Côte d'Azur
Florence
Madrid
Costa Brava
Rome
Istanbul
Algarve
Balearic Islands
Ægean Islands
Costa del Sol
Costa Blanca
Ionian Islands
Athens
Rhodes
Crete

WEALTH

The value of total production divided by population (US $, 2014)

- Over $50,000 per person
- $40,000 – 50,000 per person
- $30,000 – 40,000 per person
- $20,000 – 30,000 per person
- $10,000 – 20,000 per person
- Under $10,000 per person

Wealthiest countries:

Luxembourg $92,000 per person
Monaco $78,700 per person
Norway $66,900 per person

Poorest countries:

Ukraine $8,700 per person
Kosovo $8,000 per person
Moldova $5,000 per person

COPYRIGHT PHILIP'S

TOURISM

Tourism receipts as a percentage of Gross National Income (2013)

- Over 10% of income from tourism
- 5 – 10% of income from tourism
- 2.5 – 5% of income from tourism
- 1 – 2.5% of income from tourism
- Under 1% of income from tourism

Tourist destinations

- ■ Cultural & historical centres
- □ Coastal resorts
- □ Ski resorts
- Centres of entertainment
- Places of pilgrimage
- Places of great natural beauty

Scale 1:10 000 000 1 cm on the map = 100 km on the ground

| 0 | 100km | 200km | 300km | 400km | 500km | 600km |

Height of the land (metres)

over 4000
2000-4000
1000-2000
400-1000
200-400
0-200
sea level
below sea level

Key to map symbols

■ Over 5,000,000 inhabitants

● 1,000,000 - 5,000,000 inhabitants

• Under 1,000,000 inhabitants

<u>Helsinki</u> Capital cities underlined

Country boundaries

Locator map

COPYRIGHT PHILIP'S

Height of the land (metres)

over 4000
2000-4000
1000-2000
400-1000
200-400
0-200
below sea level

sea level

Key to map symbols

● Over 5,000,000 inhabitants

● 1,000,000 – 5,000,000 inhabitants

• Under 1,000,000 inhabitants

Paris Capital cities underlined

Country boundaries

Locator map

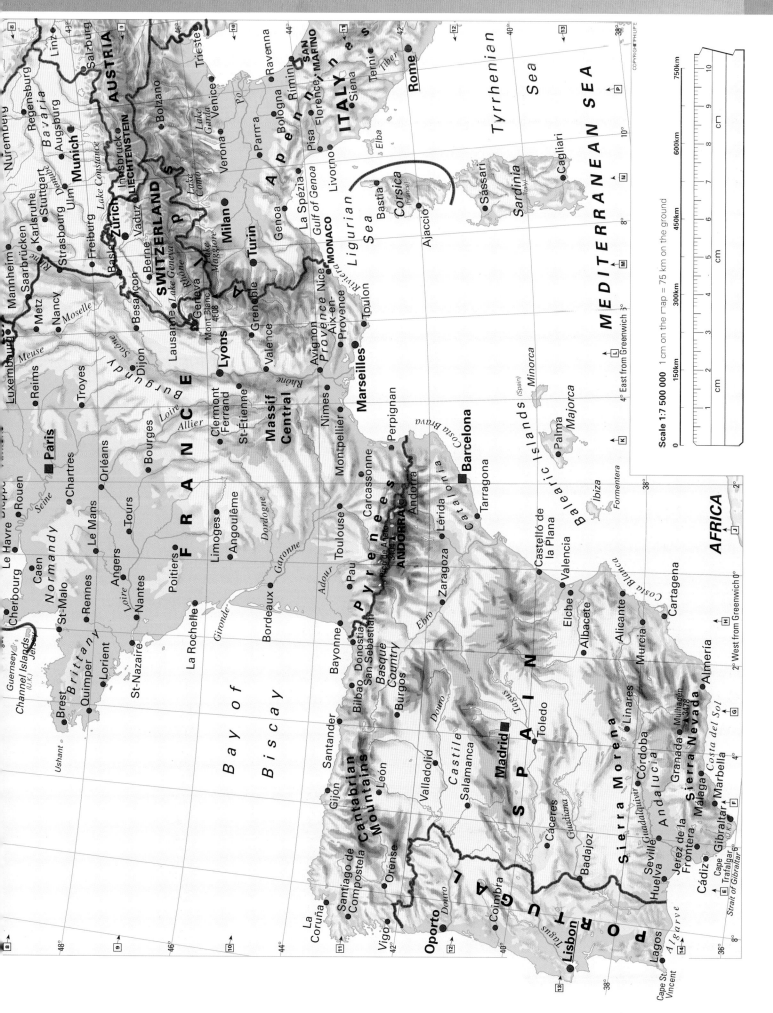

FRANCE, SPAIN and PORTUGAL

Scale 1:7 500 000   1 cm on the map = 75 km on the ground

0   150km   300km   450km   600km   750km

ATLANTIC OCEAN

IRELAND
WALES
ENGLAND
Birmingham
Cardiff
Bristol
Plymouth
Thames
Channel Islands (U.K.)
English Channel
NETHERLANDS
The Hague
Amsterdam
Rotterdam
Antwerpen
BELGIUM
Lille
Brussels
Le Havre
LUXEMBOURG
Luxembourg
Hamburg
Szczecin
Bremen
Hanover
Berlin
GERMANY
Dortmund
Cologne
Bonn
Leipzig
Dresden
Frankfurt
Mannheim
Prague
CZECH
Nuremberg
Stuttgart

London

Brest
Paris
Rennes
Seine
Nancy
Strasbourg
Munich
Linz

Bay of Biscay

Nantes
Loire
Orléans
Tours
Dijon
Clermont Ferrand
Limoges
FRANCE
Basle
Zürich
Berne
SWITZERLAND
Geneva
LIECHTENSTEIN
AUSTRIA
Lake Geneva
Lyons
St. Etienne
Mont Blanc 4808
Massif Central
Grenoble
Milan
Turin
Verona
Venice
Ljubljana
SLOVENIA
Trieste
Lake Garda

La Coruña
Vigo
Gijón
Santander
Cantabrian Mountains
Bilbao
León
Burgos
Pic d'Aneto 3404
Pyrenees
ANDORRA
Toulouse
Montpellier
MONACO
Nice
Marseilles
Toulon
Riviera
Genoa
Parma
Po
Apennines
Bologna
Florence
Pisa
Siena
Rímini
SAN MARINO
Adriatic
Gran Sasso 2914
Tiber

Oporto
Douro
PORTUGAL
Salamanca
Valladolid
Douro
Zaragoza
Ebro
Catalonia
Costa Brava
Barcelona
Corsica (France)
Ajaccio
Rome
ITALY
Mount Vesuvius 1281
Naples
Pompeii

Lisbon
Tagus
Guadiana
Badajoz
SPAIN
Madrid
Toledo
Tagus
Valencia
Balearic Islands (Spain)
Minorca
Palma
Majorca
Ibiza
Sardinia (Italy)
Cágliari
Tyrrhenian Sea

Algarve
Seville
Sierra Morena
Guadalquivir
Cordoba
Granada
Mulhacén 3478
Murcia
Alicante
Cartagena
Costa Blanca
MEDITERRANEAN

Cádiz
Málaga
Costa del Sol
Almeria
Tangier
Gibraltar (U.K.)
Strait of Gibraltar
Ceuta (Spain)
Melilla (Spain)
Tétouan
Oran
Mostaganem
Algiers
Blida
Bejaïa
Annaba
Bizerte
Carthage
Tunis
Palermo
Strómboli
Etna 3340
Sicily
Catán

Fès
Ifrane
Oujda
MOROCCO
Atlas Mountains
Constantine
ALGERIA
Sousse

AFRICA
Biskra
Chott Melrhir
TUNISIA
Sfax
Chott Djerid
Djerba
Sahara Desert

Tripoli
Al Aziziyah
LIBYA

Height of the land (metres)
- over 4000
- 2000-4000
- 1000-2000
- 400-1000
- 200-400
- 0-200
- sea level
- below sea level

Key to map symbols
- ■ Over 5,000,000 inhabitants
- ● 1,000,000 - 5,000,000 inhabitants
- • Under 1,000,000 inhabitants
- <u>Sofia</u> Capital cities underlined
- Country boundaries
- Historical sites
- Seasonal lakes

Scale 1:10 000 000   1 cm on the map = 100 km on the ground

0 — 250km — 500km — 750km — 1000km

Cross-section along latitude 45°N

Locator map

▲ **Strómboli** Known as the 'Lighthouse of the Mediterranean' it is one of three active volcanoes in Italy. The others are Mount Etna and Mount Vesuvius.

Scale 1:6 250 000   1 cm on the map = 62.5 km on the ground

0   62.5km   125km   187.5km   250km   312.5km   375km

Locator map

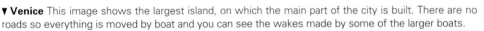

▼ **Venice** This image shows the largest island, on which the main part of the city is built. There are no roads so everything is moved by boat and you can see the wakes made by some of the larger boats.

REGIONS

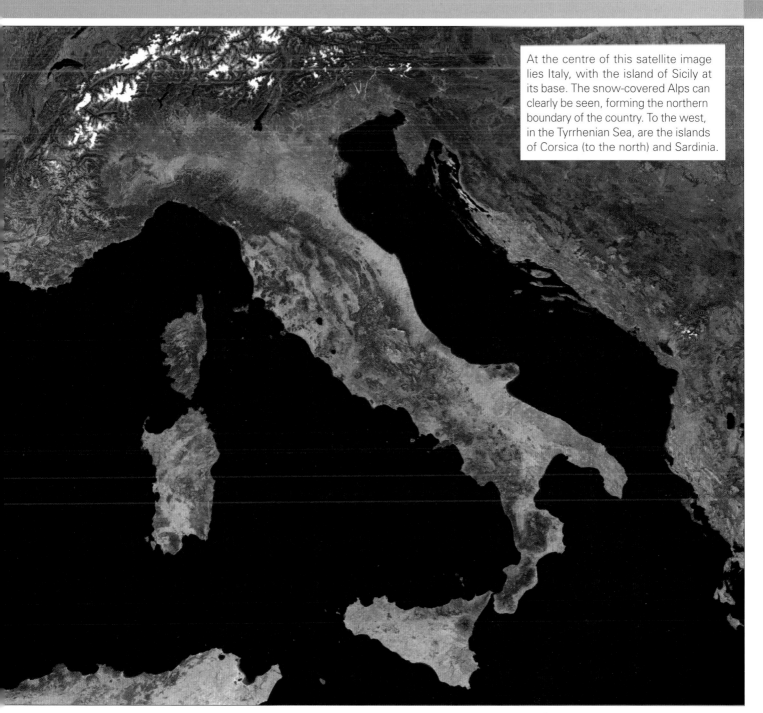

At the centre of this satellite image lies Italy, with the island of Sicily at its base. The snow-covered Alps can clearly be seen, forming the northern boundary of the country. To the west, in the Tyrrhenian Sea, are the islands of Corsica (to the north) and Sardinia.

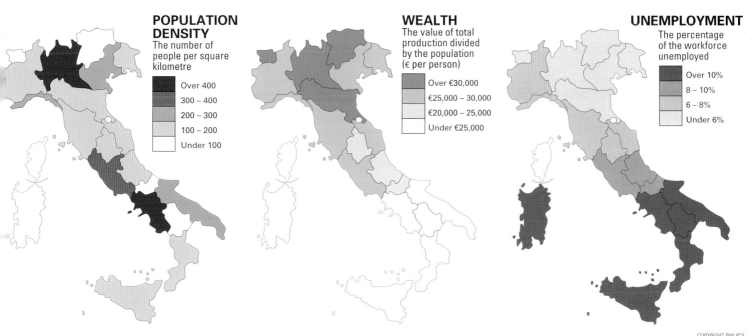

POPULATION DENSITY
The number of people per square kilometre

- Over 400
- 300 – 400
- 200 – 300
- 100 – 200
- Under 100

WEALTH
The value of total production divided by the population (€ per person)

- Over €30,000
- €25,000 – 30,000
- €20,000 – 25,000
- Under €25,000

UNEMPLOYMENT
The percentage of the workforce unemployed

- Over 10%
- 8 – 10%
- 6 – 8%
- Under 6%

COPYRIGHT PHILIP'S

Height of the land (metres)

over 4000
3000–4000
2000–3000
1000–2000
400–1000
200–400
0–200
below sea level

sea level

Locator map

North America
Arctic Ocean
Pacific Ocean
Oceania
Europe
Africa
Indian Ocean

Scale 1:48 000 000

COPYRIGHT PHILIP'S

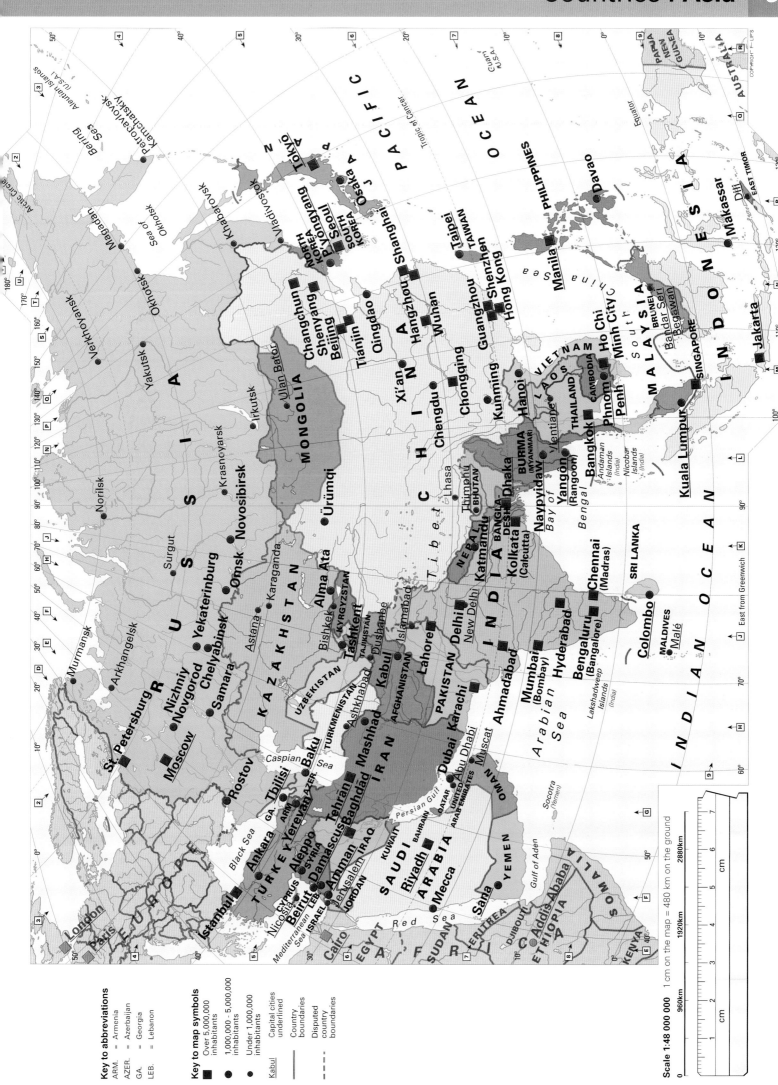

Key to abbreviations

ARM. = Armenia
AZER. = Azerbaijan
GA. = Georgia
LEB. = Lebanon

Key to map symbols

■ Over 5,000,000 inhabitants

● 1,000,000 - 5,000,000 inhabitants

• Under 1,000,000 inhabitants

Kabul Capital cities underlined

—— Country boundaries

- - - Disputed country boundaries

Scale 1:48 000 000   1 cm on the map = 480 km on the ground

Height of the land (metres)

over 6000
4000-6000
2000-4000
1000-2000
400-1000
200-400
0-200
below sea level
sea level

Key to map symbols

■ Over 5,000,000 inhabitants

● 1,000,000 - 5,000,000 inhabitants

• Under 1,000,000 inhabitants

Kiev   Capital cities underlined

···· Country boundaries

Scale 1:20 000 000   1 cm on the map = 200 km on the ground

| 0 | 500km | 1000km | 1500km | 2000km | 2500km |

COPYRIGHT PHILIP'S

Locator map

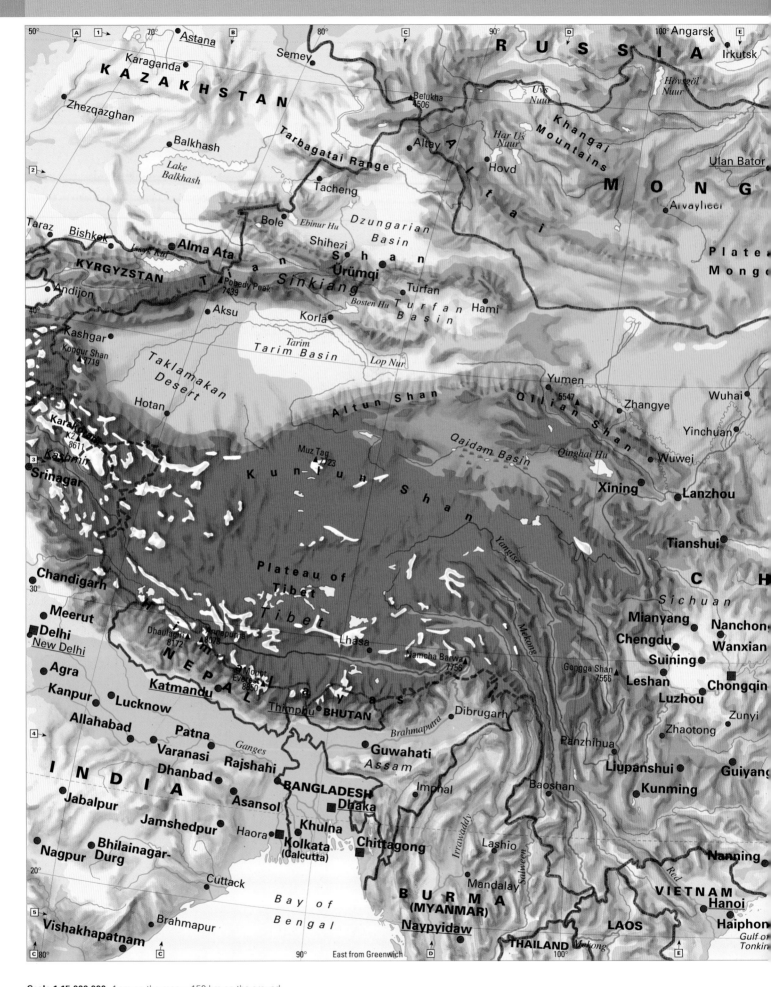

50° A 1 70° B 80° C 90° D 100° Angarsk E

R U S S I A Irkutsk

Astana

Karaganda

K A Z A K H S T A N

Zhezqazghan

Semey

Belukha 4506

Altay

Hövsgöl Nuur

Uvs Nuur

Khangai Mountains

M O N G

Balkhash

Lake Balkhash

Tarbagatai Range

Tacheng

Hovd

Har Us Nuur

Arvayheer

Ulan Bator

Plate Mongo

Taraz

Bishkek

KYRGYZSTAN

Andijon

Bole

Ebinur Hu

Shihezi

Ürümqi

Turfan

Dzungarian Basin

Tian Shan

Sinkiang

Hami

Alma Ata

Issyk Kul

Pobedy Peak 7439

Turfan Basin

Aksu

Korla

Bosten Hu

40°

Kashgar

Kongur Shan 7719

Tarim

Tarim Basin

Lop Nur

Altun Shan

Yumen 5547

Qilian Shan

Zhangye

Wuhai

Yinchuan

Taklamakan Desert

Hotan

Qaidam Basin

Qinghai Hu

Wuwei

Xining

Lanzhou

Karakoram K2 8611

Kashmir

Srinagar

Muz Tag 6973

K u n l u n   S h a n

Tianshui

Chandigarh

30°

Meerut

Delhi

New Delhi

Agra

Kanpur

Lucknow

Allahabad

Patna

Varanasi

Rajshahi

Dhanbad

I N D I A

Jabalpur

Jamshedpur

Bhilainagar-Durg

Nagpur

Plateau of Tibet

Tibet

Dhaulagiri 8172

Annapurna 8078

H i m a l a y a s

NEPAL

Katmandu

Mount Everest 8850

Thimphu

BHUTAN

Lhasa

Yangtse

Namcha Barwa 7756

Mekong

Gongga Shan 7556

S i c h u a n

Mianyang

Chengdu

Suining

Leshan

Luzhou

Nanchon

Wanxian

Chongqin

Zunyi

Zhaotong

Dibrugarh

Brahmaputra

Assam

Guwahati

Imphal

Panzhihua

Liupanshui

Guiyang

Kunming

Baoshan

Haora

Kolkata (Calcutta)

Khulna

Dhaka

BANGLADESH

Asansol

Cuttack

Chittagong

Irrawaddy

Lashio

Mandalay

Salween

Nanning

VIETNAM

Hanoi

20°

Brahmapur

Vishakhapatnam

B a y   o f   B e n g a l

B U R M A (MYANMAR)

Naypyidaw

THAILAND

LAOS

Mekong

Red

Haiphon

Gulf of Tonkin

C 80° C 90° East from Greenwich D 100° E

0   300km   600km   900km   1200km   1500km

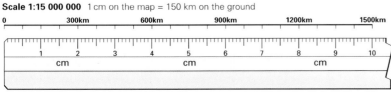

Height of the land (metres)

	over 6000
	4000-6000
	2000-4000
	1000-2000
	400-1000
	200-400
	0-200
sea level	below sea level

Locator map

Key to map symbols

■ Over 5,000,000 inhabitants

● 1,000,000 - 5,000,000 inhabitants

• Under 1,000,000 inhabitants

<u>Beijing</u> Capital cities underlined

▬ ▬ Country boundaries

▬ ▪ ▬ Disputed country boundaries

COPYRIGHT PHILIP'S

INDUSTRIAL REGIONS

Core industrial regions
- Major centres for industry
- Centres for iron and steel, and chemicals
- Rapidly developing coastal regions
- Special Economic Zones
- Special Administrative Regions

Outer industrial regions

Outer industrial regions with traditional heavy industry

Remote undeveloped regions

Direction of future growth

Important rail links

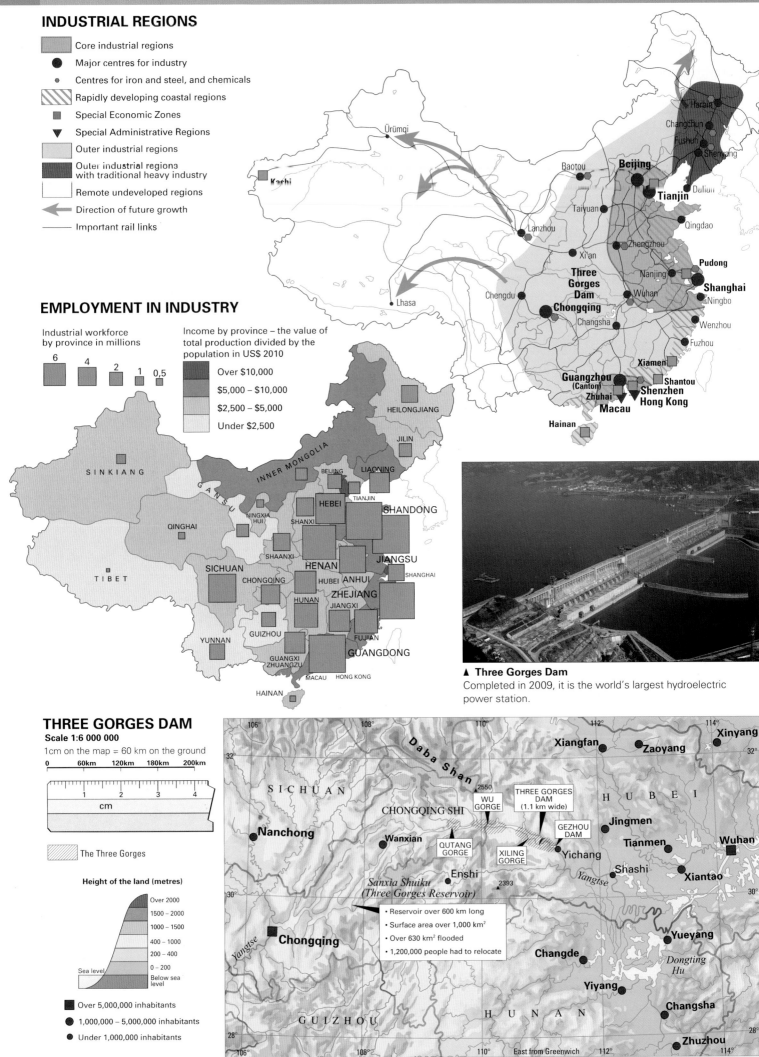

Kashi

Ürümqi

Baotou
Beijing
Tianjin
Dalian
Taiyuan
Qingdao
Lanzhou
Zhengzhou
Xi'an
Nanjing
Pudong
Three Gorges Dam
Wuhan
Shanghai
Chengdu
Chongqing
Ningbo
Changsha
Wenzhou
Fuzhou
Xiamen
Guangzhou (Canton)
Shantou
Zhuhai
Shenzhen
Macau
Hong Kong
Hainan

Harbin
Changchun
Fushun
Shenyang

EMPLOYMENT IN INDUSTRY

Industrial workforce by province in millions

6 4 2 1 0.5

Income by province – the value of total production divided by the population in US$ 2010

Over $10,000
$5,000 – $10,000
$2,500 – $5,000
Under $2,500

HEILONGJIANG

SINKIANG

JILIN

INNER MONGOLIA

GANSU

BEIJING

LIAONING

QINGHAI

NINGXIA HUI

TIANJIN

HEBEI

SHANDONG

SHANXI

TIBET

SHAANXI

HENAN

JIANGSU

SICHUAN

SHANGHAI

CHONGQING

HUBEI

ANHUI

ZHEJIANG

HUNAN

JIANGXI

YUNNAN

GUIZHOU

FUJIAN

GUANGXI ZHUANGZU

GUANGDONG

MACAU   HONG KONG

HAINAN

▲ **Three Gorges Dam**
Completed in 2009, it is the world's largest hydroelectric power station.

THREE GORGES DAM

Scale 1:6 000 000

1cm on the map = 60 km on the ground

0   60km   120km   180km   200km

| | | | |
|1|2|3|4|

cm

The Three Gorges

Height of the land (metres)

Over 2000
1500 – 2000
1000 – 1500
400 – 1000
200 – 400
0 – 200
Sea level
Below sea level

■ Over 5,000,000 inhabitants
● 1,000,000 – 5,000,000 inhabitants
• Under 1,000,000 inhabitants

Daba Shan

SICHUAN

Xinyang

Xiangfan
Zaoyang

2550

THREE GORGES DAM (1.1 km wide)

WU GORGE

CHONGQING SHI

HUBEI

Nanchong

Wanxian

QUTANG GORGE

GEZHOU DAM

Jingmen

Tianmen

Wuhan

Yichang

XILING GORGE

Shashi

Enshi

2393

Yangtse

Xiantao

Sanxia Shuiku (Three Gorges Reservoir)

- Reservoir over 600 km long
- Surface area over 1,000 km²
- Over 630 km² flooded
- 1,200,000 people had to relocate

Yueyang

Chongqing

Changde

Dongting Hu

Yangtse

Yiyang

GUIZHOU

HUNAN

Changsha

Zhuzhou

East from Greenwich

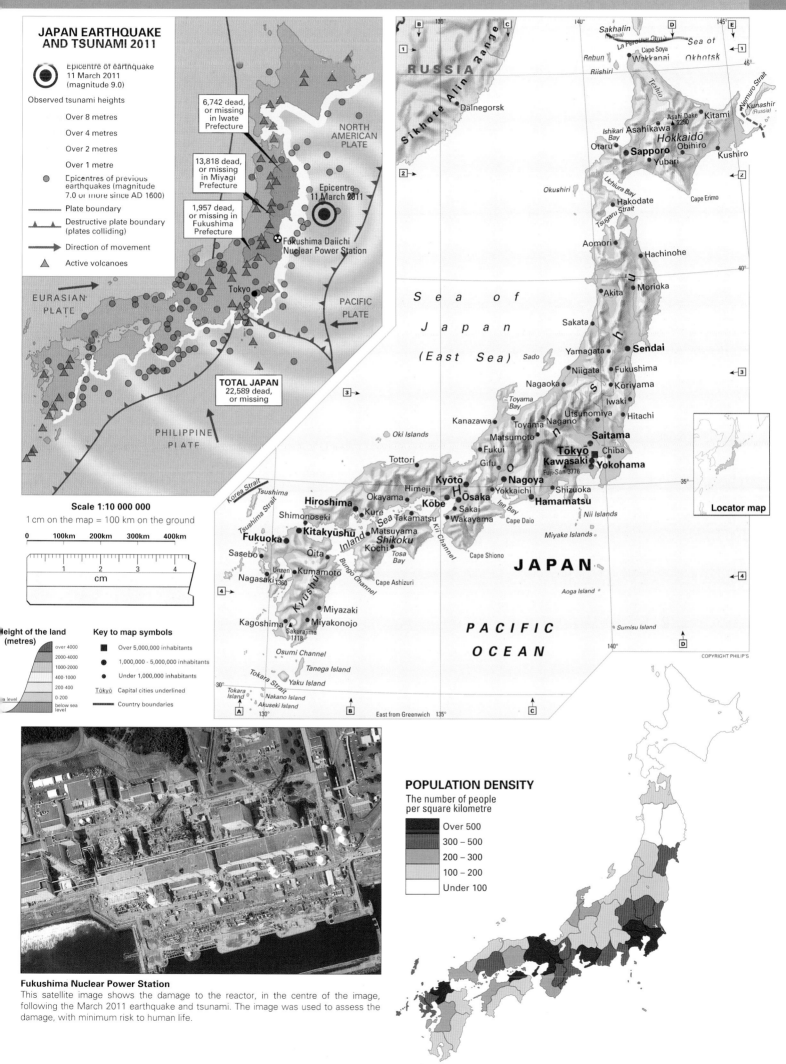

JAPAN EARTHQUAKE AND TSUNAMI 2011

- Epicentre of earthquake 11 March 2011 (magnitude 9.0)

Observed tsunami heights
- Over 8 metres
- Over 4 metres
- Over 2 metres
- Over 1 metre
- Epicentres of previous earthquakes (magnitude 7.0 or more since AD 1600)
- Plate boundary
- Destructive plate boundary (plates colliding)
- Direction of movement
- Active volcanoes

EURASIAN PLATE

NORTH AMERICAN PLATE

PACIFIC PLATE

PHILIPPINE PLATE

6,742 dead, or missing in Iwate Prefecture

13,818 dead, or missing in Miyagi Prefecture

1,957 dead, or missing in Fukushima Prefecture

Epicentre 11 March 2011

Fukushima Daiichi Nuclear Power Station

Tokyo

TOTAL JAPAN
22,589 dead, or missing

Scale 1:10 000 000

1 cm on the map = 100 km on the ground

0   100km   200km   300km   400km

cm

Height of the land (metres)
- over 4000
- 2000-4000
- 1000-2000
- 400-1000
- 200-400
- 0-200
- sea level
- below sea level

Key to map symbols
- Over 5,000,000 inhabitants
- 1,000,000 - 5,000,000 inhabitants
- Under 1,000,000 inhabitants
- Tōkyō Capital cities underlined
- Country boundaries

RUSSIA

Sikhote Alin Range

Dalnegorsk

Sakhalin (Russia)

La Perouse Strait

Cape Soya

Sea of Okhotsk

Rebun

Wakkanai

Riishiri

Rishiri

Asahi Dake 2290

Kitami

Kunashir (Russia)

Nemuro Strait

Ishikari Asahikawa
Bay

Hokkaidō

Otaru **Sapporo** Obihiro

Yubari

Kushiro

Okushiri

Uchiura Bay

Hakodate

Cape Erimo

Tsugaru Strait

Aomori

Hachinohe

Akita

Morioka

S e a   o f

J a p a n

(E a s t   S e a)

Sado

Sakata

Yamagata **Sendai**

Niigata Fukushima

Nagaoka Kōriyama

Iwaki

Utsunomiya Hitachi

Kanazawa Nagano

Toyama Bay

Toyama

Matsumoto

Saitama

Fukui

Tōkyō Chiba

Gifu **Kawasaki** **Yokohama**

Fuji-San 3776

Tottori

Kyōto **Nagoya**

Himeji **Ōsaka** Yokkaichi Shizuoka

Okayama **Kōbe** Sakai **Hamamatsu**

Hiroshima Takamatsu Wakayama

Shimonoseki Kure Sea Ise Bay Cape Daio

Kitakyūshū Matsuyama Inland **Shikoku** Kii Channel Nii Islands

Fukuoka Ōita Kōchi Miyake Islands

Sasebo Tosa Bay

Nagasaki Kumamoto Cape Ashizuri Cape Shiono

Unzen 1360 Bungo Channel

J A P A N

Miyazaki

Kagoshima Miyakonojo

Sakurajima 1118

Aoga Island

Osumi Channel Tanega Island

P A C I F I C

O C E A N

Sumisu Island

Tokara Strait

Yaku Island

Tokara Island Nakano Island

Akuseki Island

East from Greenwich 135°

Oki Islands

Korea Strait

Tsushima

Tsushima Strait

Kyūshū

Locator map

COPYRIGHT PHILIP'S

Fukushima Nuclear Power Station

This satellite image shows the damage to the reactor, in the centre of the image, following the March 2011 earthquake and tsunami. The image was used to assess the damage, with minimum risk to human life.

POPULATION DENSITY

The number of people per square kilometre
- Over 500
- 300 – 500
- 200 – 300
- 100 – 200
- Under 100

TURKEY
Beirut
LEBANON
Tel Aviv-Jaffa
ISRAEL
Jerusalem
Aleppo
SYRIA
Damascus
Ammn
JORDAN
Cairo
EGYPT
Nile
Mesopotamia
Mosul
Tigris
Euphrates
IRAQ
Baghdd
Basra
Abadan
KUWAIT
Kuwait
Al Manmah
BAHRAIN
Al Hufuf
QATAR
Doha
Dubai
Abu Dhabi
UNITED ARAB EMIRATES
Yerevan
ARMENIA
AZERBAIJAN
Baku
Caspian Sea
Tabrz
Tehrn
IRAN
Mashnad
Esfahn
Shirz
Kermn
Zagros Mountains
Persian Gulf
Gulf of Oman
Muscat
OMAN

Medina
Jedda
Mecca
SAUDI ARABIA
Riyadh
Red Sea
Nafud Desert
Rub 'al Khl
(Empty Quarter)
Sana
YEMEN
Aden
Gulf of Aden
Al Mukall
DJIBOUTI
SOMALIA
Ras Asir
Socotra
(Yemen)
AFRICA

KAZAKHSTAN
Karaganda
Aral Sea
Syrdarya
Lake Balkhash
Dzungaria
Altai
Ürümqi
UZBEKISTAN
Kara Kum
Amudarya
Samarkand
TURKMENISTAN
Ashkhabad
Dushanbe
TAJIKISTAN
Bishkek
Alma Ata
KYRGYZSTAN
Papedy Peak 7439
Tashkent
Ismail Samani Peak
Tian Shan
Tarim
Taklamakan Desert
Kunlun Shan
Herat
AFGHANISTAN
Kbul
Hindu Kush
Kandahr
Quetta
Kashmir
K2 8611
Karakoram
Srinagar
Plateau of Tibet
Islamabad
Lahore
Amritsar
Multan
Faisalabad
Punjab
PAKISTAN
Indus
CHINA
Lhasa
Himalayas

Thar Desert
Delhi
New Delhi
Agra
Jaipur
Kanpur
Lucknow
Allahabad
Varanasi
Dhaulagiri 8172
Mount Everest 8850
Katmandu
NEPAL
Ganges
Patna
BHUTAN
Thimphu
Brahmaputra
Assam
Mawsynram
BANGLADESH
Dhaka
Chittagong

Karachi
Hyderabad
Ahmadabad
Rajkot
Vadodara
Surat
INDIA
Indore
Jabalpur
Jamshedpur
Nagpur
Kolkata
(Calcutta)

Mumbai
(Bombay)
Pune
Godavari
Solapur
Hyderabad
Goa
Western Ghats
Krishna
Eastern Ghats
Deccan
Vishakhapatnam
Bay of Bengal

Arabian Sea

Lakshadweep Islands
(India)

Bengaluru
(Bangalore)
Chennai
(Madras)
Coimbatore
Tiruchchirappalli
Cochin
Madurai
Jaffna
Cape Comorin
Colombo
SRI LANKA

Andaman Islands
(India)

Nicobar Islands
(India)

Scale comparison map
U.K and Ireland
on same scale

MALDIVES
Malé

Chagos Archipelago
(U.K.)

SEYCHELLES
Victoria

INDIAN OCEAN
Equator

Scale 1:27 500 000   1cm on the map = 275 km on the ground
0   550km   1100km   1650km   2200km   2750km

1 2 3 4 5 6 7 8 9 10
cm   cm   cm

60°   70°   East from Greenwich   80°   90°

Cross-section along latitude 30°N

IRAN   PAKISTAN   INDIA   TIBET   CHINA

Himalayas
Brahmaputra
Mount Everest 8850
Persian Gulf
Zagros Mountains
Indus Chenab Sutlej
Ganges
Tibetan Plateau
Salween Mekong Yangtse
Yangtse   Yangtse Yangtse
East China Sea
30°N

Height of the land (metres)

	over 6000
	4000-6000
	2000-4000
	1000-2000
	400-1000
	200-400
	0-200
sea level	
	below sea level

Locator map

Key to map symbols

■ Over 5,000,000 inhabitants

● 1,000,000 - 5,000,000 inhabitants

• Under 1,000,000 inhabitants

Beijing Capital cities underlined

▬▬▬ Country boundaries

▬ ▬ ▬ Disputed country boundaries

Seasonal lakes

COPYRIGHT PHILIP'S

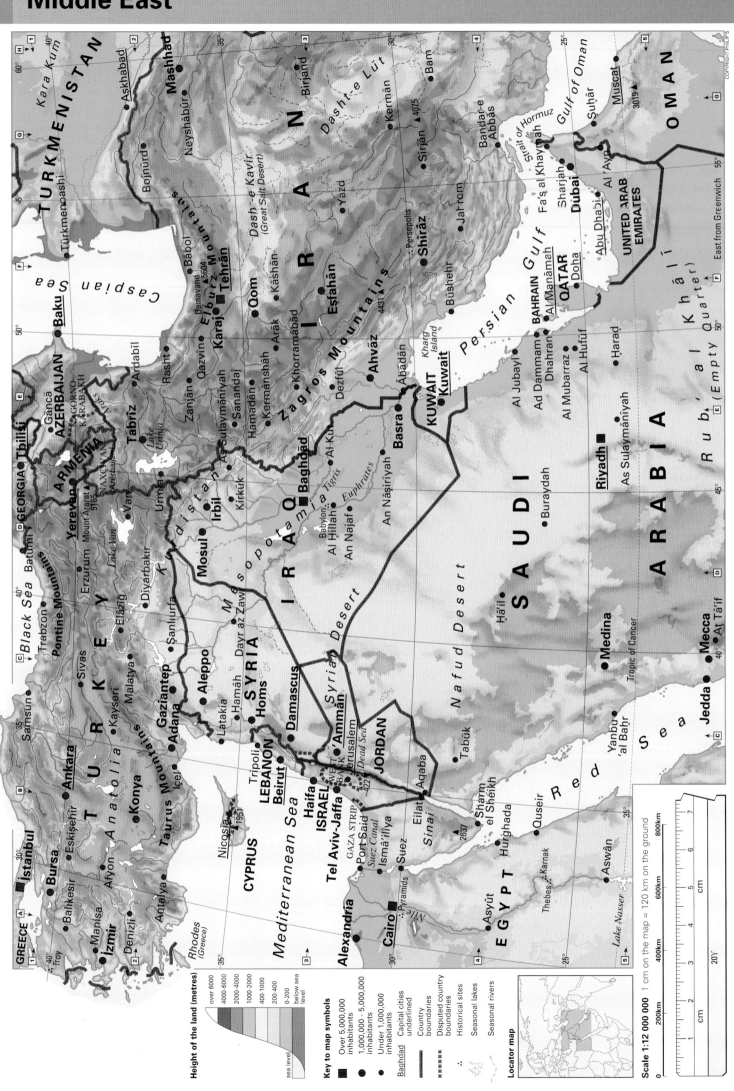

Height of the land (metres)

over 6000
4000-6000
2000-4000
1000-2000
400-1000
200-400
0-200
below sea level

sea level

Key to map symbols

■ Over 5,000,000 inhabitants
● 1,000,000 - 5,000,000 inhabitants
• Under 1,000,000 inhabitants

Baghdad   Capital cities underlined

——— Country boundaries
------ Disputed country boundaries
∴∴ Historical sites
—— Seasonal lakes
—— Seasonal rivers

Locator map

Scale 1:12 000 000   1 cm on the map = 120 km on the ground

0   200km   400km   600km   800km

0   1   2   3   4   5   6   7
cm

20Ý

COPYRIGHT PHILIP'S

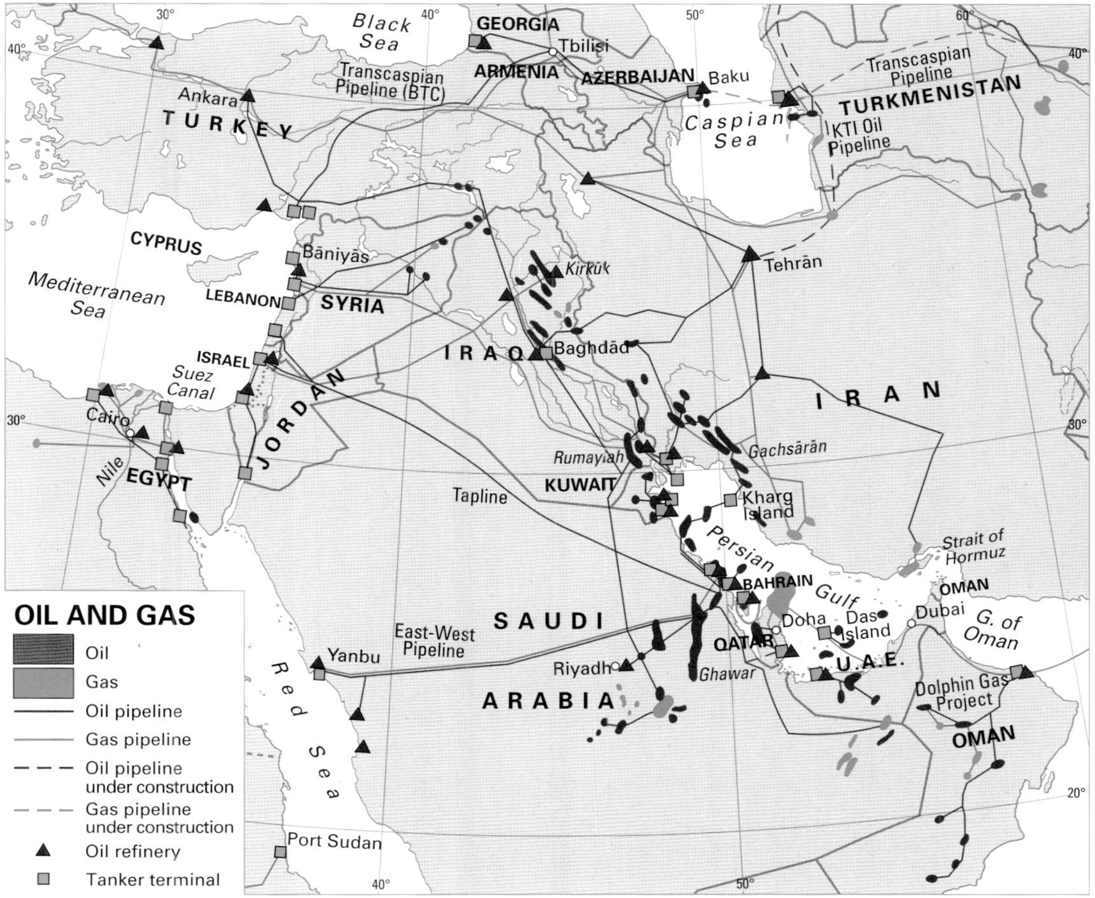
OIL AND GAS
Oil
Gas
Oil pipeline
Gas pipeline
Oil pipeline under construction
Gas pipeline under construction
Oil refinery
Tanker terminal
Black Sea
GEORGIA
Tbilisi
ARMENIA
AZERBAIJAN
Baku
Transcaspian Pipeline (BTC)
Transcaspian Pipeline
TURKMENISTAN
KTI Oil Pipeline
Caspian Sea
Ankara
TURKEY
CYPRUS
Bāniyās
Mediterranean Sea
LEBANON
SYRIA
Kirkūk
Tehrān
ISRAEL
Suez Canal
IRAQ
Baghdād
Cairo
JORDAN
IRAN
Nile
EGYPT
Rumayiah
Gachsārān
KUWAIT
Tapline
Kharg Island
Strait of Hormuz
Persian Gulf
BAHRAIN
OMAN
SAUDI
Doha
Das Island
Dubai
G. of Oman
East-West Pipeline
QATAR
U.A.E.
Yanbu
Riyadh
Ghawar
ARABIA
Dolphin Gas Project
OMAN
Red Sea
Port Sudan

Top 10 oil producers

(thousand barrels per day 2014)

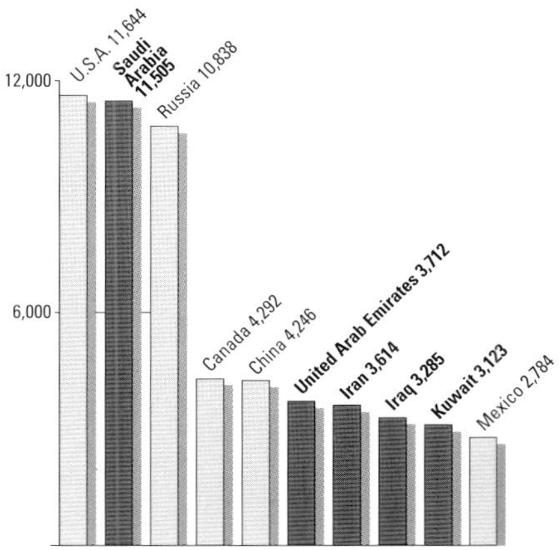
12,000
6,000
U.S.A. 11,644
Saudi Arabia 11,505
Russia 10,838
Canada 4,292
China 4,246
United Arab Emirates 3,712
Iran 3,614
Iraq 3,285
Kuwait 3,123
Mexico 2,784

Oil production by region

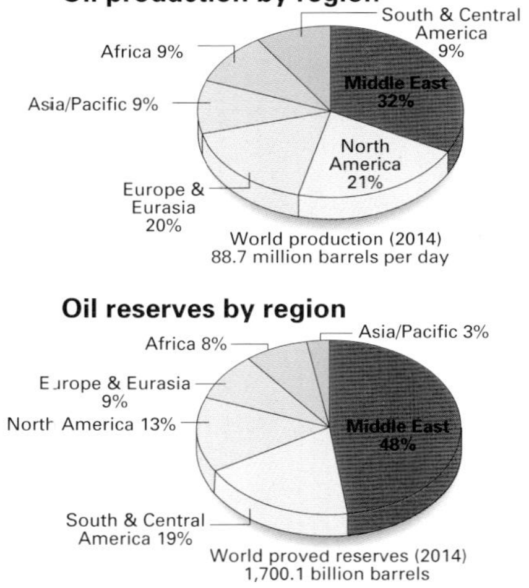
South & Central America 9%
Africa 9%
Middle East 32%
Asia/Pacific 9%
North America 21%
Europe & Eurasia 20%
World production (2014) 88.7 million barrels per day
Oil reserves by region
Africa 8%
Asia/Pacific 3%
Europe & Eurasia 9%
North America 13%
Middle East 48%
South & Central America 19%
World proved reserves (2014) 1,700.1 billion barrels

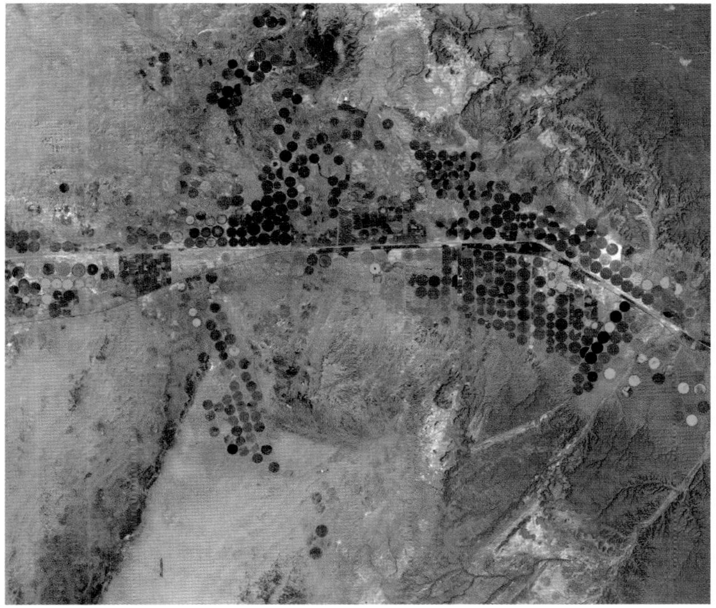

◀ Riyadh, Saudi Arabia
This satellite image shows the area near the capital, Riyadh. The city is set in an arid landscape and the water supply for the city and agriculture is extracted from underground reservoirs or 'aquifers'. The green circles are fields, irrigated by centre-pivot watering systems.

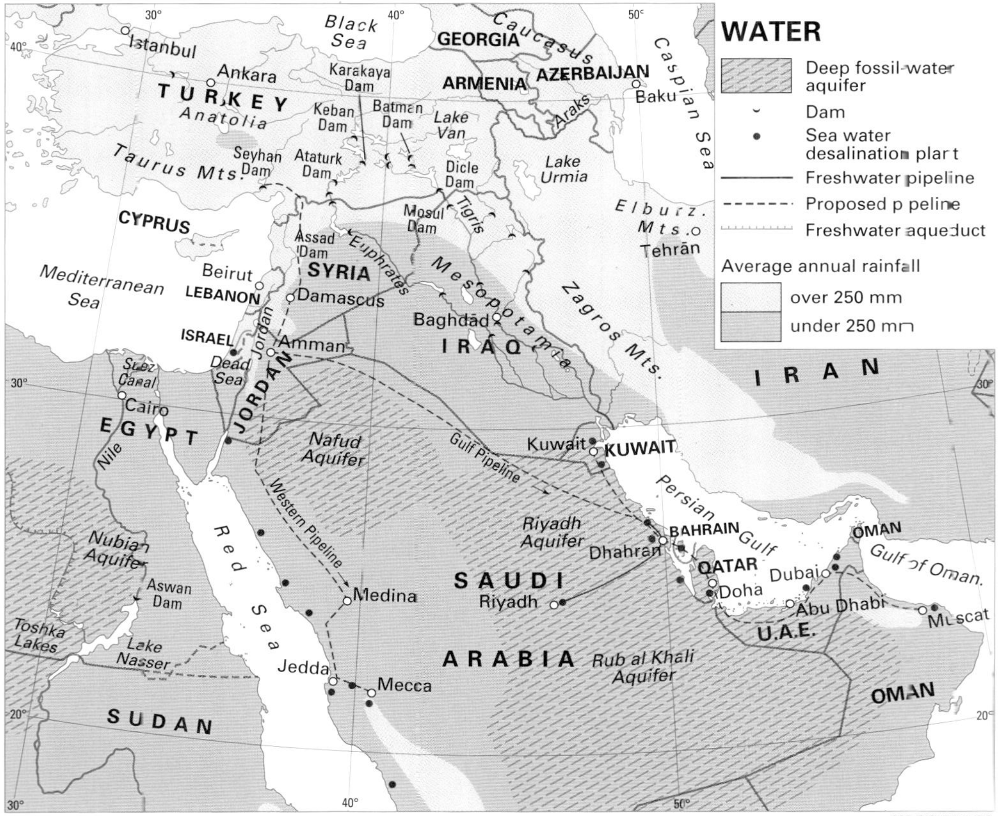
WATER
Deep fossil-water aquifer
Dam
Sea water desalination plant
Freshwater pipeline
Proposed pipeline
Freshwater aqueduct
Average annual rainfall
over 250 mm
under 250 mm
Istanbul
Black Sea
GEORGIA
Caucasus
Caspian Sea
Ankara
Karakaya Dam
ARMENIA
AZERBAIJAN
Baku
TURKEY
Anatolia
Keban Dam
Batman Dam
Lake Van
Araks
Taurus Mts.
Seyhan Dam
Ataturk Dam
Dicle Dam
Lake Urmia
Tigris
Mosul Dam
Elburz Mts.
Tehrān
CYPRUS
Assad Dam
Euphrates
Beirut
SYRIA
Mesopotamia
Mediterranean Sea
LEBANON
Damascus
Baghdad
Zagros Mts.
ISRAEL
Jordan
Amman
IRAQ
Dead Sea
IRAN
Suez Canal
Cairo
JORDAN
EGYPT
Nafud Aquifer
Gulf Pipeline
Kuwait
KUWAIT
Nile
Western Pipeline
Persian Gulf
Riyadh Aquifer
BAHRAIN
Dhahran
Nubian Aquifer
Red Sea
OMAN
Gulf of Oman
QATAR
Doha
Dubai
Aswan Dam
SAUDI
Riyadh
Medina
Abu Dhabi
Muscat
Toshka Lakes
Lake Nasser
Jedda
ARABIA
Rub al Khali Aquifer
U.A.E.
Mecca
OMAN
SUDAN

COPYRIGHT PHILIP'S

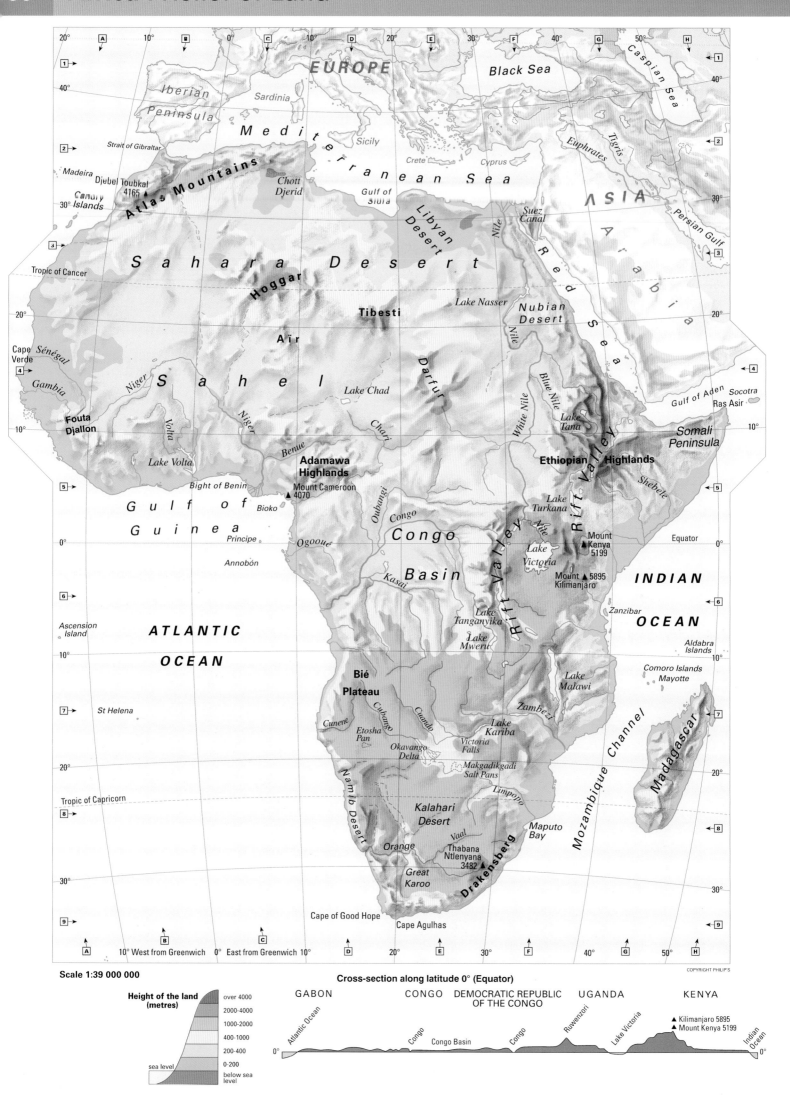

Scale 1:39 000 000

Height of the land
(metres)

over 4000
2000-4000
1000-2000
400-1000
200-400
0-200
below sea
level

sea level

Cross-section along latitude 0° (Equator)

GABON   CONGO   DEMOCRATIC REPUBLIC   UGANDA   KENYA
OF THE CONGO

Atlantic Ocean   Congo   Congo Basin   Congo   Ruwenzori   Lake Victoria   ▲ Kilimanjaro 5895   ▲ Mount Kenya 5199   Indian Ocean

COPYRIGHT PHILIP'S

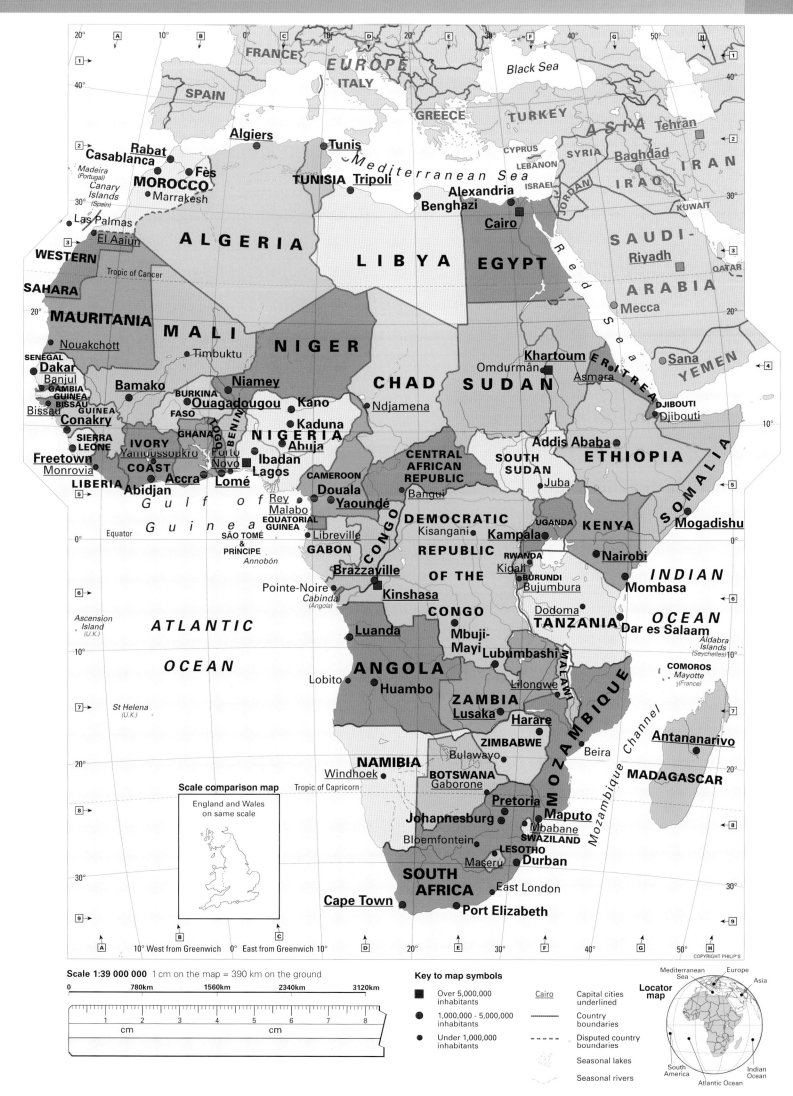

FRANCE EUROPE
ITALY Black Sea
SPAIN
GREECE TURKEY ASIA
Algiers CYPRUS SYRIA Tehrān
Rabat Tunis Mediterranean Sea LEBANON IRAQ Baghdād IRAN
Casablanca ISRAEL
Madeira Fès TUNISIA Tripoli Alexandria JORDAN
(Portugal) MOROCCO Benghazi KUWAIT
Canary Marrakesh Cairo SAUDI- Riyadh
Islands QATAR
(Spain) Las Palmas ARABIA
El Aaiún Tropic of Cancer Mecca
WESTERN ALGERIA LIBYA EGYPT
SAHARA
Red Sea
MAURITANIA MALI NIGER Sana
Nouakchott Khartoum ERITREA YEMEN
SENEGAL Timbuktu Omdurmân
Dakar Asmara
Banjul Bamako CHAD SUDAN DJIBOUTI
GAMBIA Niamey Djibouti
GUINEA- BURKINA Kano Ndjamena
Bissau BISSAU Ouagadougou Kaduna Addis Ababa
Conakry FASO SOUTH ETHIOPIA
GUINEA GHANA NIGERIA SUDAN
SIERRA Yamoussoukro Ahuja CENTRAL Juba SOMALIA
LEONE IVORY Porto Ibadan AFRICAN
Freetown COAST Novo Lagos REPUBLIC
Monrovia Accra Lomé CAMEROON Bangui
LIBERIA Abidjan Douala DEMOCRATIC Mogadishu
Gulf of Rey Yaoundé
Malabo REPUBLIC UGANDA KENYA
Guinea EQUATORIAL Libreville Kisangani Kampala
GUINEA OF THE Nairobi
Equator SÃO TOMÉ GABON RWANDA INDIAN
& Kigali
PRÍNCIPE Brazzaville CONGO BURUNDI Mombasa
Annobón Bujumbura OCEAN
Pointe-Noire Kinshasa Dodoma
Ascension Cabinda CONGO TANZANIA Dar es Salaam
Island (Angola) Mbuji- Aldabra
(U.K.) ATLANTIC Luanda Mayi Lubumbashi Islands
(Seychelles)
OCEAN ANGOLA COMOROS
Lobito Mayotte
Huambo Lilongwe (France)
St Helena ZAMBIA Antananarivo
(U.K.) Lusaka Harare
Beira
ZIMBABWE MOZAMBIQUE MADAGASCAR
NAMIBIA Bulawayo
Windhoek BOTSWANA Tropic of Capricorn
Gaborone Maputo
Pretoria Mbabane
Johannesburg SWAZILAND
Bloemfontein LESOTHO
Maseru Durban
SOUTH East London
Cape Town AFRICA
Port Elizabeth

Scale comparison map

England and Wales
on same scale

Mozambique Channel

COPYRIGHT PHILIP'S

Scale 1:39 000 000   1 cm on the map = 390 km on the ground

0	780km	1560km	2340km	3120km

cm   cm

Key to map symbols

◼ Over 5,000,000 inhabitants   Cairo   Capital cities underlined

● 1,000,000 - 5,000,000 inhabitants   ———   Country boundaries

· Under 1,000,000 inhabitants   - - - -   Disputed country boundaries

Seasonal lakes

Seasonal rivers

Mediterranean Sea   Europe
Locator map   Asia

South   Indian
America   Ocean
Atlantic Ocean

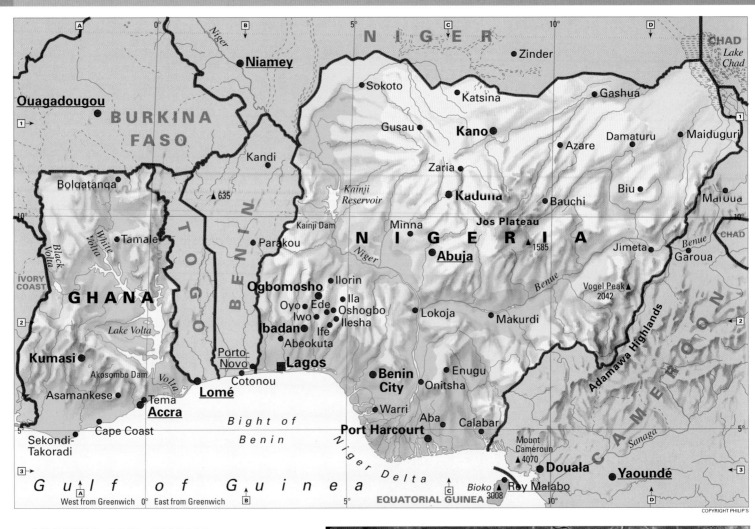

COPYRIGHT PHILIP'S

NIGERIA AND GHANA

Scale 1:10 000 000 1 cm on the map = 100 km on the ground

0   100km   200km   300km   400km   500km   600km

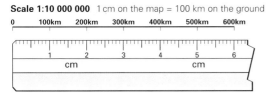

1   2   3   4   5   6
cm   cm

See page opposite for key to map symbols, locator map and height of the land reference panel.

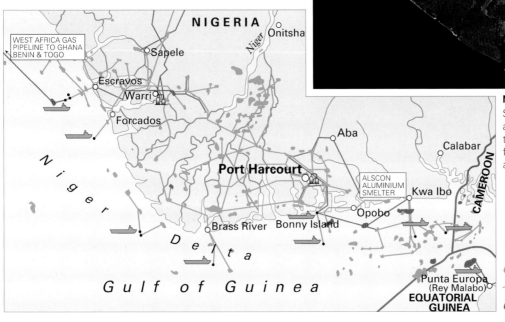

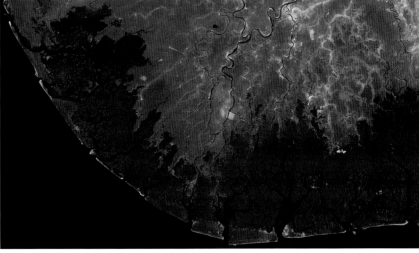

Niger Delta, Nigeria ▲

Satellite imagery helps to plan the drilling for oil and gas in the delta and to monitor the effect of the drilling on this fragile environment. This is a false colour image which shows vegetation such as mangrove swamps in dark red.

OIL AND GAS IN THE NIGER DELTA

Oilfields	Gas pipelines
Oil pipelines	Tanker terminals
Gasfields	Oil refineries

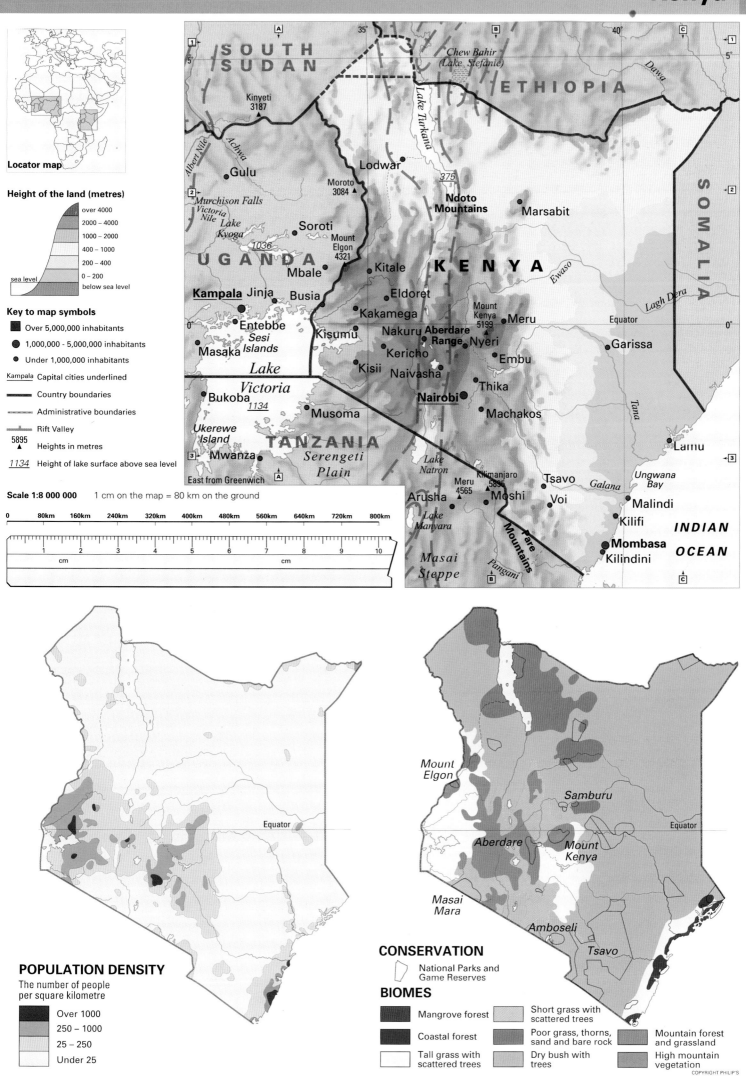

Locator map

Height of the land (metres)

- over 4000
- 2000 – 4000
- 1000 – 2000
- 400 – 1000
- 200 – 400
- 0 – 200
- sea level
- below sea level

Key to map symbols

- Over 5,000,000 inhabitants
- 1,000,000 – 5,000,000 inhabitants
- Under 1,000,000 inhabitants

Kampala Capital cities underlined

— Country boundaries

--- Administrative boundaries

⋯ Rift Valley

▲ 5895 Heights in metres

1134 Height of lake surface above sea level

Scale 1:8 000 000   1 cm on the map = 80 km on the ground

0   80km 160km 240km 320km 400km 480km 560km 640km 720km 800km

cm   cm

POPULATION DENSITY

The number of people
per square kilometre

- Over 1000
- 250 – 1000
- 25 – 250
- Under 25

CONSERVATION

National Parks and
Game Reserves

BIOMES

- Mangrove forest
- Coastal forest
- Tall grass with scattered trees
- Short grass with scattered trees
- Poor grass, thorns, sand and bare rock
- Dry bush with trees
- Mountain forest and grassland
- High mountain vegetation

COPYRIGHT PHILIP'S

Cross-section along longitude 147°E

AUSTRALIA

North

Great Barrier Reef

Great Divide

Darling

Mount Kosciuszko 2228

Murray

Snowy Mountains

Bass Strait

Tasmania

South

147°E

147°E

Height of the land (metres)

over 4000
2000-4000
1000-2000
400-1000
200-400
0-200
sea level
below sea level

Key to map symbols

Over 5,000,000 inhabitants

1,000,000 - 5,000,000 inhabitants

Under 1,000,000 inhabitants

Canberra Capital cities underlined

Country boundaries

State boundaries

Seasonal lakes

Seasonal rivers

Locator map

Asia

Pacific Ocean

Indian Ocean

Southern Ocean

Antarctica

East from Greenwich

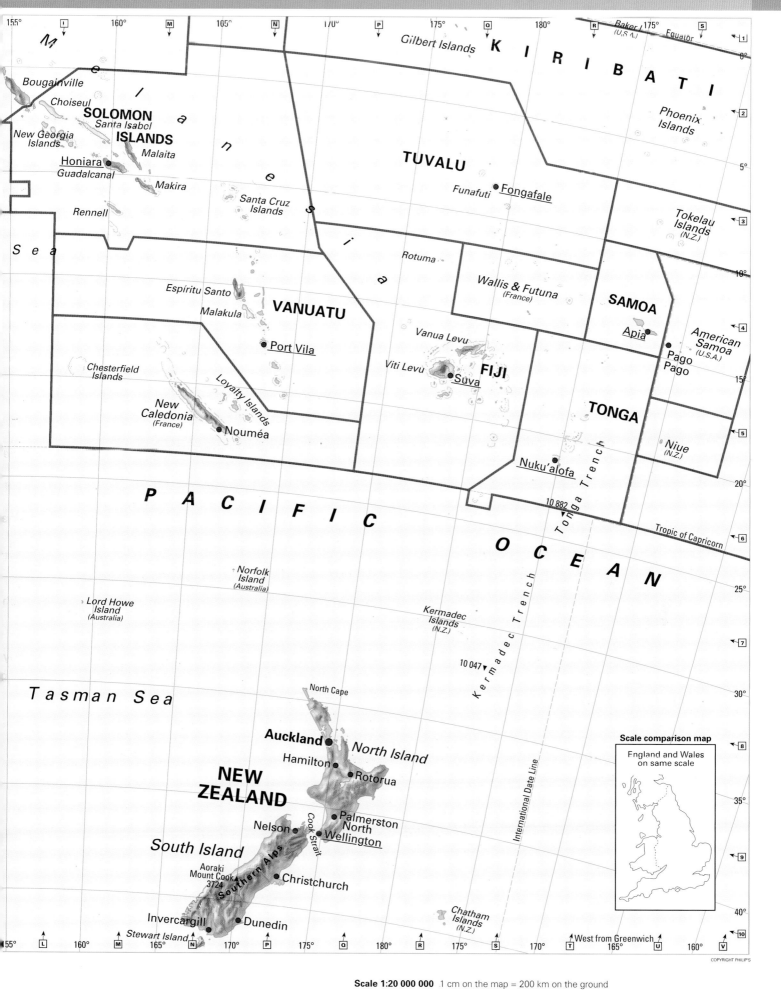

Scale 1:20 000 000 1 cm on the map = 200 km on the ground

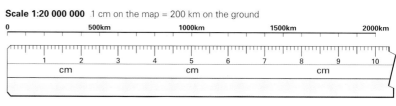

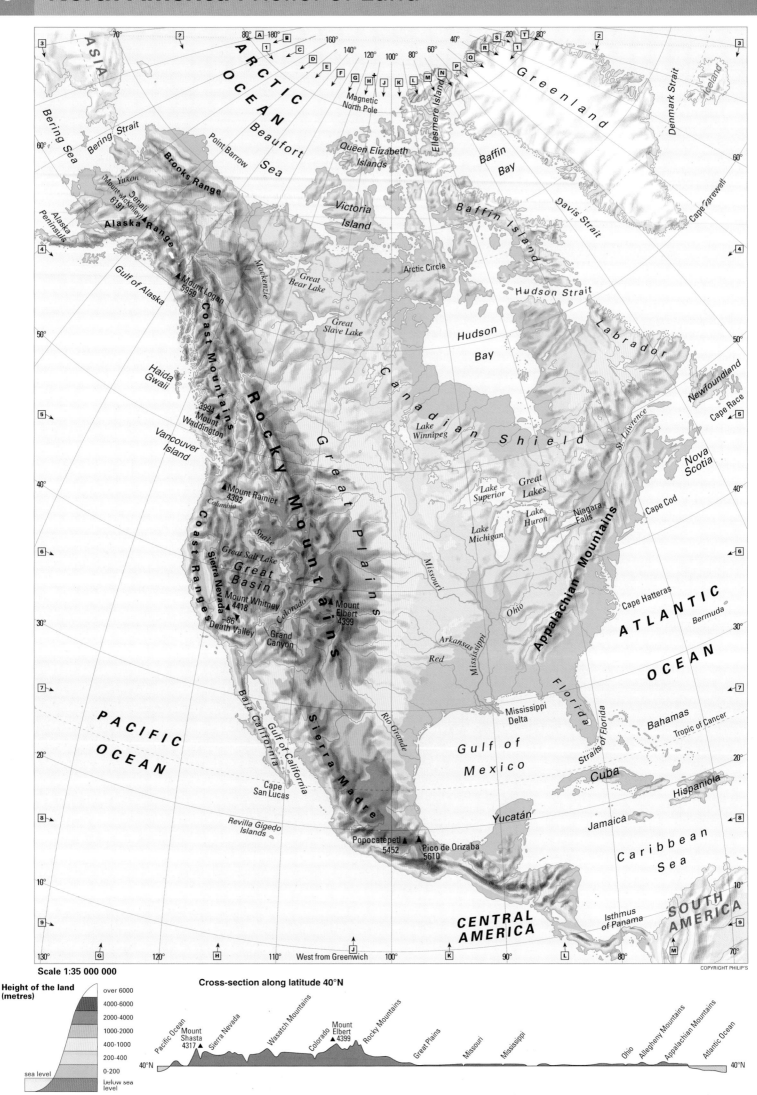

Scale 1:35 000 000

COPYRIGHT PHILIP'S

Height of the land (metres)

over 6000
4000–6000
2000–4000
1000–2000
400–1000
200–400
0–200
below sea level

sea level

Cross-section along latitude 40°N

Pacific Ocean — Mount Shasta 4317 — Sierra Nevada — Wasatch Mountains — Colorado — Mount Elbert 4399 — Rocky Mountains — Great Plains — Missouri — Mississippi — Ohio — Allegheny Mountains — Appalachian Mountains — Atlantic Ocean

40°N

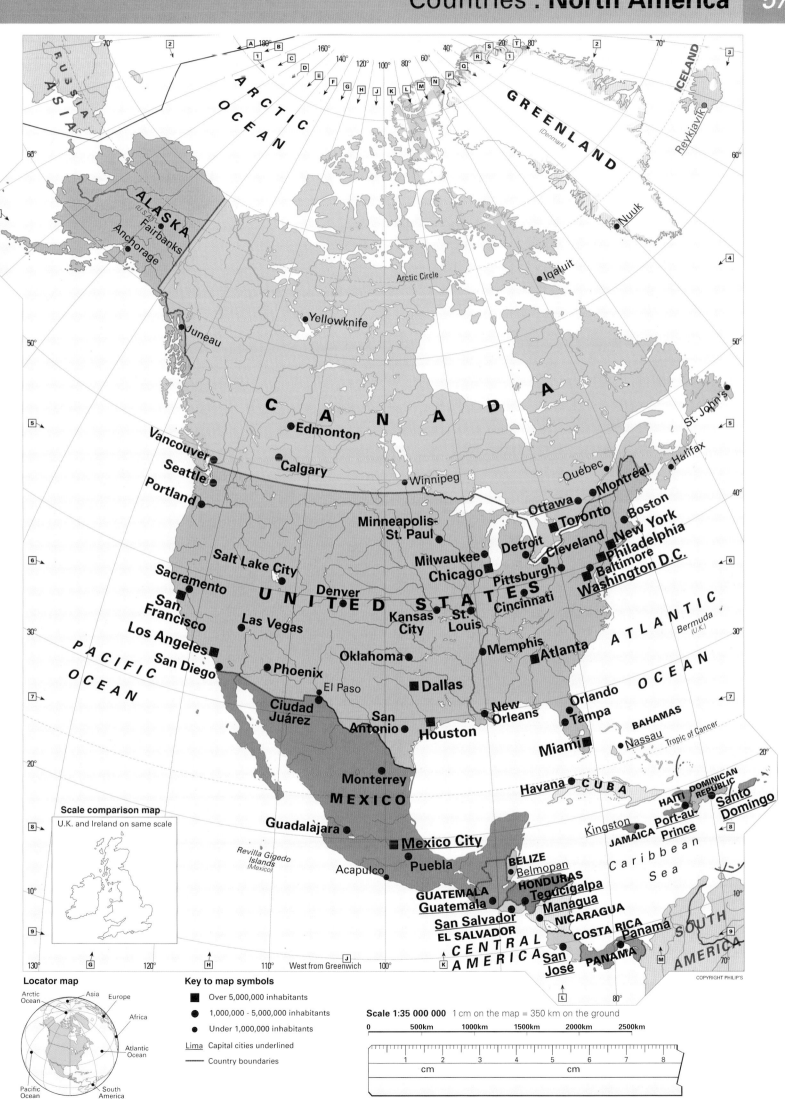

Scale comparison map
U.K. and Ireland on same scale

Revilla Gigedo
Islands
(Mexico)

Locator map

Arctic
Ocean

Asia
Europe

Africa

Atlantic
Ocean

Pacific
Ocean

South
America

Key to map symbols

■ Over 5,000,000 inhabitants

● 1,000,000 – 5,000,000 inhabitants

• Under 1,000,000 inhabitants

<u>Lima</u> Capital cities underlined

—— Country boundaries

Scale 1:35 000 000   1 cm on the map = 350 km on the ground

0	500km	1000km	1500km	2000km	2500km

COPYRIGHT PHILIP'S

cm

cm

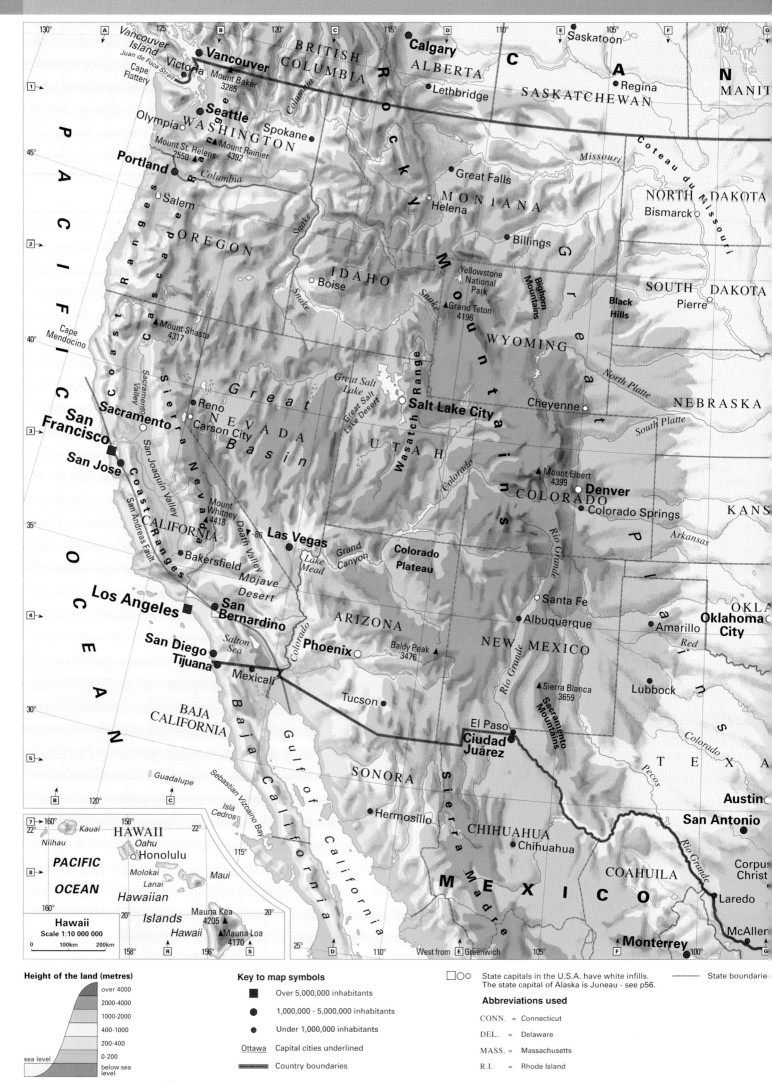

Height of the land (metres)

over 4000
2000-4000
1000-2000
400-1000
200-400
0-200
below sea level

sea level

Key to map symbols

■ Over 5,000,000 inhabitants

● 1,000,000 - 5,000,000 inhabitants

• Under 1,000,000 inhabitants

Ottawa Capital cities underlined

Country boundaries

□○○ State capitals in the U.S.A. have white infills.
The state capital of Alaska is Juneau - see p.56.

Abbreviations used

CONN. = Connecticut

DEL. = Delaware

MASS. = Massachusetts

R.I. = Rhode Island

State boundaries

Hawaii
Scale 1:10 000 000
0   100km   200km

Scale 1:12 000 000   1cm on the map = 120 km on the ground

0   200km   400km   600km   800km   1000km   1200km

Locator map

IRRIGATION

Total irrigation per state
(million gallons per day)

Over 30,000

10,000

5000

1000

Under 1000

Irrigation is the watering of the land and crops by means of canals, ditches, pipes and wells. The biggest source of water for irrigation is that which has percolated into natural underground reservoirs or 'aquifers'. It can be extracted using either wells or pumps and, although replenished naturally, is at risk through overuse and depletion

Areas with more than 10% of irrigated land

TOURISM

Tourist centres

Concentration of hotels

National Parks

WA
ID
MT
ND
ME
OR
MN
VT NH
MA
SD
WI
NY
RI
CT
NV
WY
MI
PA
NJ
CA
UT
NE
IA
OH
MD DE
IL
IN
WV
VA
CO
KS
KY
WA
NM
MO
NC
AZ
OK
AR
TN
SC
MS
AL
GA
TX
LA
FL

Olympic
North Cascades
Seattle
Glacier
Mount Rainier
Voyageurs
Isle Royale
Acad
Theodore Roosevelt
Crater Lake
Yellowstone
Badlands
Minneapolis
Niagara Falls
Bos
Redwood
Grand Teton
Wind Cave
Detroit
New
Lassen Volcanic
San Francisco
Great Basin
Chicago
Philadelphia
Atlantic
Yosemite
Capitol Reef
Arches
Rocky Mountains
Washington D
Kings Canyon
Bryce Canyon
Denver
Saint Louis
Shenandoah
Sequoia
Canyonlands
Kansas City
Great Smoky Mountains
Death Valley
Zion
Mesa Verde
Channel Islands
Las Vegas
Grand Canyon
Mammoth Cave
Los Angeles
Petrified Forest
Phoenix
San Diego
Saguaro
Atlanta
Carlsbad Caverns
Hot Springs
Dallas
Guadalupe Mountains
New Orleans
Big Bend
Houston
Orlando
Tampa
Everglades
Miami
Dry Tortugas

Central business district

Urban area

Park and open space

State boundary

Freeway

Other road

✈ Airport

▪ Place of interest

NEW YORK

1cm on the map = 25 km on the ground

Scale 1:250 000

0   2km   4km   6km   8km   10km

Lodi
Bogota
74°00'
Bedford Park
73°50'
The Cloisters
Hasbrouck Heights
Ridgefield Park
Leonia
Fordham University
Botanical Gardens
TETERBORO AIRPORT
Little Ferry
Palisades Park
Fort Lee
Washington Heights
Bronx Zoo
Westchester
Carlstadt
Ridgefield
George Washington Bridge
Tremont
40°50'
Cliffside Park
Yankee Stadium
40°50'
Meadowlands
Fairview
Melrose
Throgs Neck
North Bergen
Harlem
Bronx
East River
Whitestone
Secaucus
American Museum of Natural History
Rikers Island
College Point
West New York
Lincoln Center
Central Park
Astoria
LA GUARDIA AIRPORT
Flushing
Weehawken
Metropolitan Museum of Art
East Elmhurst
Citi Field
Union City
Rockefeller Center
Long Island City
National Tennis Center
Flushing Meadows-Corona Park
Hoboken
Empire State Building
United Nations Headquarters
Jackson Heights
Elmhurst
Meadow Lake
Manhattan
Greenwich Village
East River
Rego Park
Forest Hills
Lincoln Park
New York University
Middle Village
Forest Hills
Jersey City
I WTC
Woodhaven
Richmond Hill
NEWARK AIRPORT
Wall Street
Ridgewood
Aqueduct Race Track
Statue of Liberty
Ellis Island
Bedford-Stuyvesant
Ozone Park
Bayonne
Governors Island
South Brooklyn
East New York
40°40'
Upper New York Bay
Prospect Park
Brooklyn Botanic Gardens
40°40'
JFK INT. AIRPORT
New Brighton
Borough Park
Flatbush
Howard Beach
Staten Island
Stapleton
The Narrows
Bay Ridge
New Utrecht
Bensonhurst
Brooklyn
Jamaica
Gateway National Recreation Area
Verrazano Narrows Bridge
Sheepshead Bay
Marine Park
Bay
Lower New York Bay
Coney Island
Coney Island Beach
New York Aquarium
Inlet
Rockway Park
Midland Beach
Hoffman Island
West from Greenwich
74°00'
73°50'

Hudson River
Hackensack River
NEW JERSEY
NEW YORK
COPYRIGHT PHILIP'S

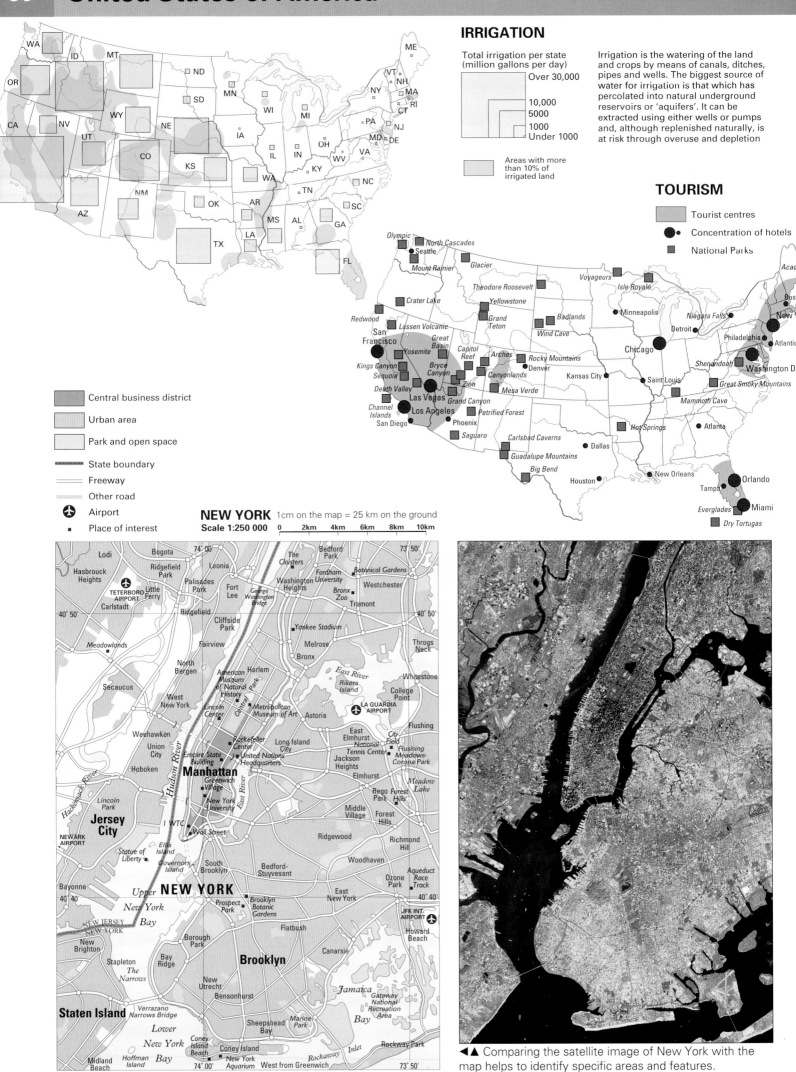

◀▲ Comparing the satellite image of New York with the map helps to identify specific areas and features.

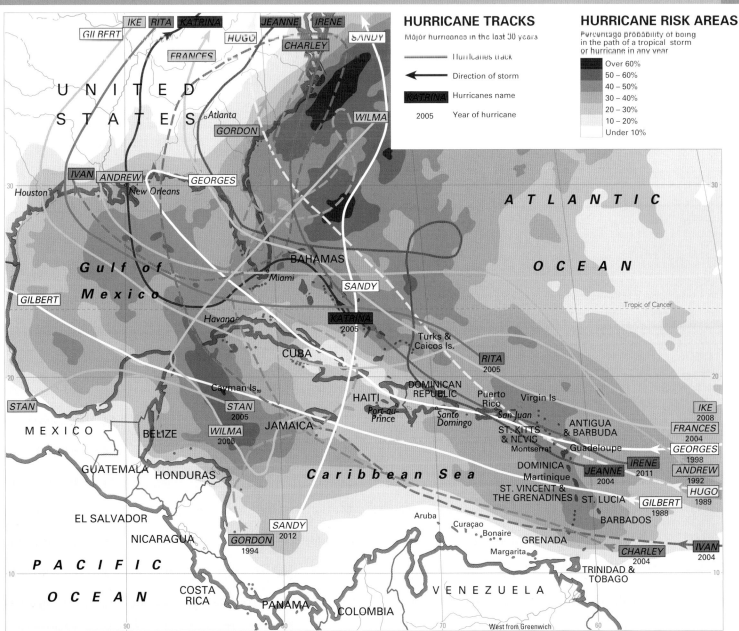

HURRICANE TRACKS

Major hurricanes in the last 30 years

Hurricanes track

← Direction of storm

KATRINA Hurricanes name

2005 Year of hurricane

HURRICANE RISK AREAS

Percentage probability of being in the path of a tropical storm or hurricane in any year

- Over 60%
- 50 – 60%
- 40 – 50%
- 30 – 40%
- 20 – 30%
- 10 – 20%
- Under 10%

▲ Hurricane Katrina hit the USA's Gulf Coast on 29 August 2005. It was the costliest and one of the five deadliest hurricanes ever to strike the United States. This satellite image shows the storm approaching the US coastline.

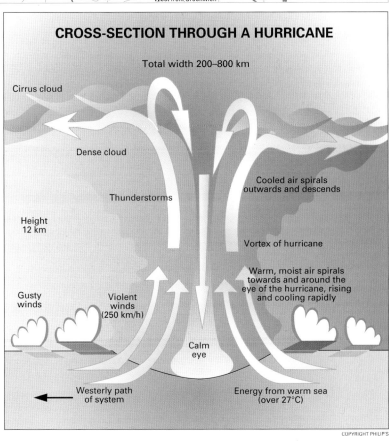

CROSS-SECTION THROUGH A HURRICANE

Total width 200–800 km

Cirrus cloud

Dense cloud

Thunderstorms

Cooled air spirals outwards and descends

Vortex of hurricane

Warm, moist air spirals towards and around the eye of the hurricane, rising and cooling rapidly

Height 12 km

Gusty winds

Violent winds (250 km/h)

Calm eye

Westerly path of system

Energy from warm sea (over 27°C)

Tijuana
Mexicali
Bataques
Phoenix
Tucson
Nogales
El Paso
Ciudad Juárez
Hermosillo
Ciudad Obregón
Chihuahua
Los Mochis
3050
Torreón
Reynosa
Monterrey
Matamoros
La Paz
Culiacán
Cabo San Lucas
Mazatlán
Durango
MEXICO
San Luis Potosí
Tampico
Aguascalientes
León
Guadalajara
Las Tres Marias
Cabo Corrientes
Querétaro
Revilla Gigedo Islands
Volcán Popocatepetl
5610
Mérida
Cancún
Cozumel
Mexico
5452
Pico de Orizaba
Campeche
Yucatán
Cuernavaca
Veracruz
Puebla
Villahermosa
Balsas
Acapulco
Oaxaca
Isthmus of Tehuantepec
Belmopan
Belize City
BELIZE
Tuxtla Gutiérrez
Chiapa
GUATEMALA
Puerto Barrios
Gulf of Tehuantepec
4093
San Pedro Sula
HONDURAS
Guatemala
Tegucigalpa
San Salvador
EL SALVADOR
NICARAG
Managua
Lake Nicaragua

UNITED STATE
Texas
Dallas
Austin
Houston
San Antonio
New Orleans
Birmingham
Corpus Christi
Nuevo Laredo
Mississippi River Delta

Rio Grande do Norte
Pecos
Conchos
Yaqui
Sonora
Sierra Madre
Aguanaval
Rio Grande de Santiago

Gulf of California
Baja California
Colorado

Gulf of Mexico
Tropic of Cancer
Gulf of Campeche
Yucatán Strait
Gulf of Honduras

PACIFIC
OCEAN

Gulf of Tehuantepec

Scale comparison map

England and Wales on same scale

West from Greenwich

Height of the land (metres)

	over 4000
	2000-4000
	1000-2000
	400-1000
	200-400
	0-200
sea level	below sea level

Key to map symbols

■ Over 5,000,000 inhabitants

● 1,000,000 - 5,000,000 inhabitants

• Under 1,000,000 inhabitants

Mexico Capital cities underlined

━━━ Country boundaries

ATLANTIC OCEAN

Atlanta

Cape Fear

Bermuda (U.K.) • Hamilton

Savannah

Jacksonville

Sargasso Sea

Orlando

Tampa

Grand Bahama Island

Fort Lauderdale • Freeport

Miami

Cape Sable

Nassau

Tropic of Cancer

Key West

Straits of Florida

BAHAMAS

Havana • Matanzas

Santa Clara

C U B A

Cienfuegos

Turks & Caicos Islands (U.K.)

Camagüey • Holguín

Santiago de los Caballeros

8605 ▼ Milwaukee Deep

Cayman Islands (U.K.)

1972 ▲ Guantanamo Bay (U.S.A.)

Santiago de Cuba

Windward Passage

3175 ▲

HAITI

DOMINICAN REPUBLIC

Mona Passage

San Juan

Virgin Islands (U.K.–U.S.A.)

ANTIGUA & BARBUDA

▲1338

Charlotte Amalie

Montego Bay

Port au Prince

2280 ▲

Santo Domingo

PUERTO RICO (U.S.A.)

St. John's

JAMAICA

Kingston

Basseterre

ST KITTS & NEVIS

Montserrat (U.K.)

Pointe-à-Pitre

GUADELOUPE (France)

Basse-Terre

Leeward Islands

DOMINICA

Roseau

MARTINIQUE (France)

Fort-de-France

Caribbean Sea

Castries

ST LUCIA

Windward Islands

Kingstown

Bridgetown

BARBADOS

ST VINCENT & THE GRENADINES

St. George's

GRENADA

ABC Islands

Aruba (Netherlands)

Curaçao (Netherlands)

Tobago

Gulf of Venezuela

Willemstad

Margarita

Port of Spain

TRINIDAD & TOBAGO

Mosquito Coast

Barranquilla

Sierra Nevada de Santa Marta

Maracaibo

Maracay

Caracas

Barcelona

Maturín

Delta of the Orinoco

Cartagena

Magdalena

Valledupar

5775 ▲

Barquisimeto

Valencia

JA

COSTA RICA

San José

Panama Canal

Isthmus of Panama

Gulf of Darién

Lake Maracaibo

4981 ▲

Panamá

3475 ▲

Montería

Orinoco

Ciudad Guayana

P A N A M A

Gulf of Panama

Cúcuta

4100 ▲

Cord. de Mérida

San Cristóbal

Ciudad Bolívar

Georgetown

V E N E Z U E L A

G U Y A N A

S U R I N A M E

Bucaramanga

Angel Falls

Mount Roraima 2810 ▲

2556 ▲

Medellín

1280 ▲

Quibdó

C O L O M B I A

Manizales • Tolima

Pereira

5215 ▲

S O U T H

Sierra Pacaraima

Essequibo

Ibagué

Bogotá

Boa Vista

Buenaventura • Palmira

Cali

Guaviare

A M E R I C A

B R A Z I L

Andes

4646 ▲

West from Greenwich

COPYRIGHT PHILIP'S

Scale 1:15 000 000   1 cm on the map = 150 km on the ground

0   300km   600km   900km   1200km   1500km

1   2   3   4   5   6   7   8   9   10

cm   cm   cm

Locator map

ATLANTIC OCEAN

Greater Antilles

Caribbean Sea

Leeward Islands

Lesser Antilles

Windward Islands

CENTRAL AMERICA

Panama Canal

Gulf of Panama

Magdalena

5775

Lake Maracaibo

Orinoco

Angel Falls

Guiana Highlands

Pico de Neblina 3014

Negro

Equator

Cotopaxi 5897

Chimborazo 6267

Galapagos Islands

Japurá

Amazon Basin

Amazon

Amazon

Selvas

Ucayali

Purus

Madeira

Tapajós

Xingu

Tocantins

Huascaran 6768

São Francisco

A   n   d   e   s

Lake Titicaca

Plateau of Mato Grosso

Lake Poopo

Brazilian Highlands

Atacama Desert

Gran Chaco

2890

Tropic of Capricorn

PACIFIC

Paraguay

Paraná

Iguaçu Falls

OCEAN

Ojos del Salado 6863

Paraná

Uruguay

Aconcagua 6962

Pampas

Colorado

Río de la Plata

ATLANTIC

A   n   d   e   s

OCEAN

Isla de Chiloé

Patagonia

Lago del Carbon -105

Falkland Islands

Strait of Magellan

Tierra del Fuego

South Georgia

Cape Horn

COPYRIGHT PHILIP'S

Height of the land (metres)

over 4000
3000 – 4000
2000 – 3000
1000 – 2000
500 – 1000
200 – 500
0 – 200
sea level
below sea level

Cross-section along latitude 20°S

CHILE   BOLIVIA   PARAGUAY   BRAZIL

▲ Ojos del Salado 6863
▲ Ancohuma & Illampu 6550

Andes

Pacific Ocean

Pilcomayo

Gran Chaco

Paraguay

Verde

Paraná

Brazilian Highlands

São Francisco

Doce

Atlantic Ocean

20°S   20°S

Scale 1:35 000 000

BAHAMAS
CUBA
MEXICO
DOMINICAN
REPUBLIC
JAMAICA   HAITI
GUATEMALA
PUERTO   ST KITTS &
HONDURAS   RICO   NEVIS
(U.S.A.)   ANTIGUA & BARBUDA
NICARAGUA   GUADELOUPE
(France)
DOMINICA
MARTINIQUE
(France)
ST LUCIA
ST VINCENT &   BARBADOS
THE GRENADINES   GRENADA

Caribbean Sea

ATLANTIC

OCEAN

COSTA
RICA   PANAMA

Barranquilla   Maracaibo
Barquisimeto   **Caracas**   TRINIDAD & TOBAGO
VENEZUELA   Ciudad
Bucaramanga   Guayana   Georgetown
Medellin   **Bogota**   **GUYANA**   Paramaribo
Cali   **COLOMBIA**   **SURINAME**   Cayenne
Boa Vista   **FRENCH
GUIANA**

Macapá   *Equator*
Quito   Belém
ECUADOR
Guayaquil   Cuenca   Manaus   São Luis
Iquitos   Santarém   Fortaleza
Trujillo   **B R A Z I L**   Teresina   Natal
Rio Branco   Pôrto Velho   João Pessao
PERU   Imperatrix   Recife
Maceió
Lima   Machu Picchu   Palmas   Aracaju
Cusco   **Salvador**

Arequipa   **La Paz**   Cuiabá   **Brasília**
BOLIVIA   Goiânia
Arica   Santa Cruz   Campo
Sucre   Grande   **Belo
Horizonte**
PACIFIC   **Vitória**
Antofagasta   **PARAGUAY**   Campinas   **Nova Iguaçu**
OCEAN   **Asunción**   São Paulo   **Rio de Janeiro**
San Miguel de   Curitiba
Tucumán   Florianopolis
San   Pôrto Alegre
Juan   Córdoba
Valparaíso   Santa   **URUGUAY**
Mendoza   Fé
Santiago   Rosario   **Montevideo**
CHILE   **Buenos Aires**
La Plata
Concepción   **ARGENTINA**   Mar del Plata
Temuco   Neuquén   Bahia Blanca   *ATLANTIC*

*Juan Fernández
(Chile)*   *OCEAN*

*Galapágos
Islands
(Ecuador)*

Falkland Islands
(U.K.)   Stanley
Punta
Arenas   South Georgia
(U.K.)

110° West from Greenwich 100°   90°   80°   70°   60°   50°   40°   30°

Scale comparison map

U.K. and Ireland
on same scale

Locator map

North America   Atlantic Ocean
Africa

Pacific
Ocean
Antarctica

Key to map symbols

■ Over 5,000,000 inhabitants

● 1,000,000 - 5,000,000 inhabitants

• Under 1,000,000 inhabitants

Lima   Capital cities underlined

------ Country boundaries

Scale 1:35 000 000   1 cm on the map = 350 km on the ground

0   500km   1000km   1500km   2000km   2500km

1   2   3   4   5   6   7
cm   cm

Locator map

ATLANTIC OCEAN

VENEZUELA
Orinoco
Boa Vista
COLOMBIA
Guiana Highlands
SURINAME
GUYANA
FRENCH GUIANA
Pico de Neblina 2994
RORAIMA
Branco
AMAPÁ
Macapá
Equator
Bragança
Belém
São Luís
Parnaíba
Negro
Uaupés
Japurá
Solimões
Içá
Putumayo
Manaus
Santarém
Amazon
Bacabal
Fortaleza
Mossoró
RIO GRANDE DO NORTE
Juruá
AMAZONAS
Selvas
Purus
Madeira
Tapajós
PARÁ
Marabá
MARANHÃO
Imperatriz
Teresina
CEARÁ
Natal
Joã Pess
Recif
Maceió
Juàzeiro do Norte
PARAÍBA
Campina Grande
PERNAMBUCO
Aripuanã
Teles Pires
Juruena
Xingu
Araguaia
Tocantins
Sobradinho Reservoir
São Francisco
Juàzeiro
ALAGOAS
Pôrto Velho
ACRE
Rio Branco
RONDÔNIA
B R A Z I L
Palmas
Aracaju
SERGIPE
Mamoré
Guaporé
BOLIVIA
MATO GROSSO
TOCANTINS
B A H Í A
Feira de Santana
Salvador
Paraguay
Cuiabá
Vitória da Conquista
Itabuna
Anápolis
Brasília
Montes Claros
Teófilo Otoni
Goiânia
GOIÁS
Uberlândia
MATO GROSSO DO SUL
MINAS GERAIS
Belo Horizonte
Pico da Bandeira 2890
ESPÍRITO SANTO
Vitória
Campo Grande
Araçatuba
SÃO PAULO
Ribeirão Prêto
Juiz de Fora
Campos
Bauru
Nova Iguaçu
Tropic of Capricorn
Paraná
Londrina
Campinas
Rio de Janeiro
São Paulo
Santos
Brazilian Highlands
PARANÁ
Ponta Grossa
Curitiba
ATLANTIC OCEAN
Foz do Iguaçu
Iguaçu
SANTA CATARINA
Joinville
Florianópolis
ARGENTINA
Caxias do Sul
RIO GRANDE DO SUL
Pôrto Alegre
West from Greenwich
Uruguaiana
Lagoa dos Patos
Pelotas
URUGUAY
PARAGUAY

Scale 1:21 000 000   1 cm on the map = 210 km on the ground

| 0 | 210km | 420km | 630km | 840km | 1050km | 1260km |

cm

Height of the land (metres)
over 4000
2000 – 4000
1000 – 2000
400 – 1000
200 – 400
0 – 200
sea level
below sea level

Key to map symbols
■ Over 5,000,000 inhabitants
● 1,000,000 – 5,000,000 inhabitants
• Under 1,000,000 inhabitants
Brasília Capital cities underlined
Country boundaries
State boundaries

WEALTH
The value of total production divided by the population in US$
Over $10,000
$7,500 – 10,000
$5,000 – 7,500
Under $5,000

COPYRIGHT PHILIP'S

POPULATION DENSITY
The number of people per square kilometre
Over 100
50 – 100
10 – 50
Under 10

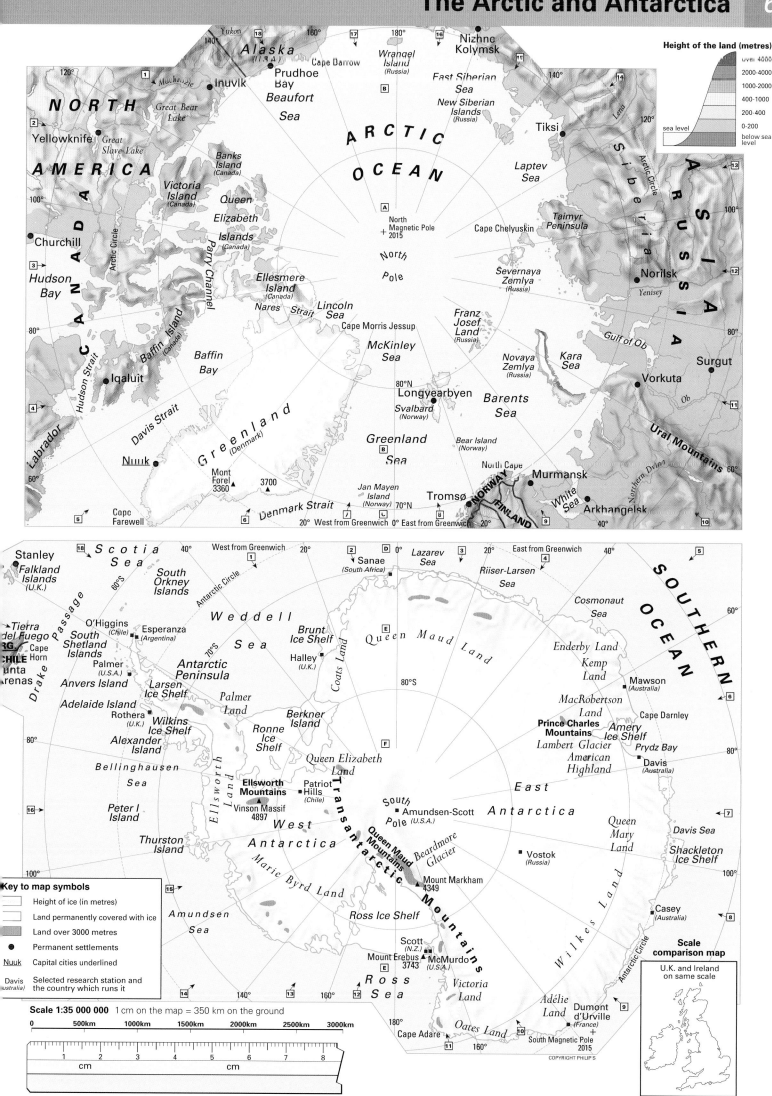

Height of the land (metres)

over 4000
2000-4000
1000-2000
400-1000
200-400
0-200
below sea level

Key to map symbols

	Height of ice (in metres)
	Land permanently covered with ice
	Land over 3000 metres
●	Permanent settlements
Nuuk	Capital cities underlined
Davis (Australia)	Selected research station and the country which runs it

Scale 1:35 000 000 1 cm on the map = 350 km on the ground

0 500km 1000km 1500km 2000km 2500km 3000km

Scale comparison map

U.K. and Ireland on same scale

COPYRIGHT PHILIP'S

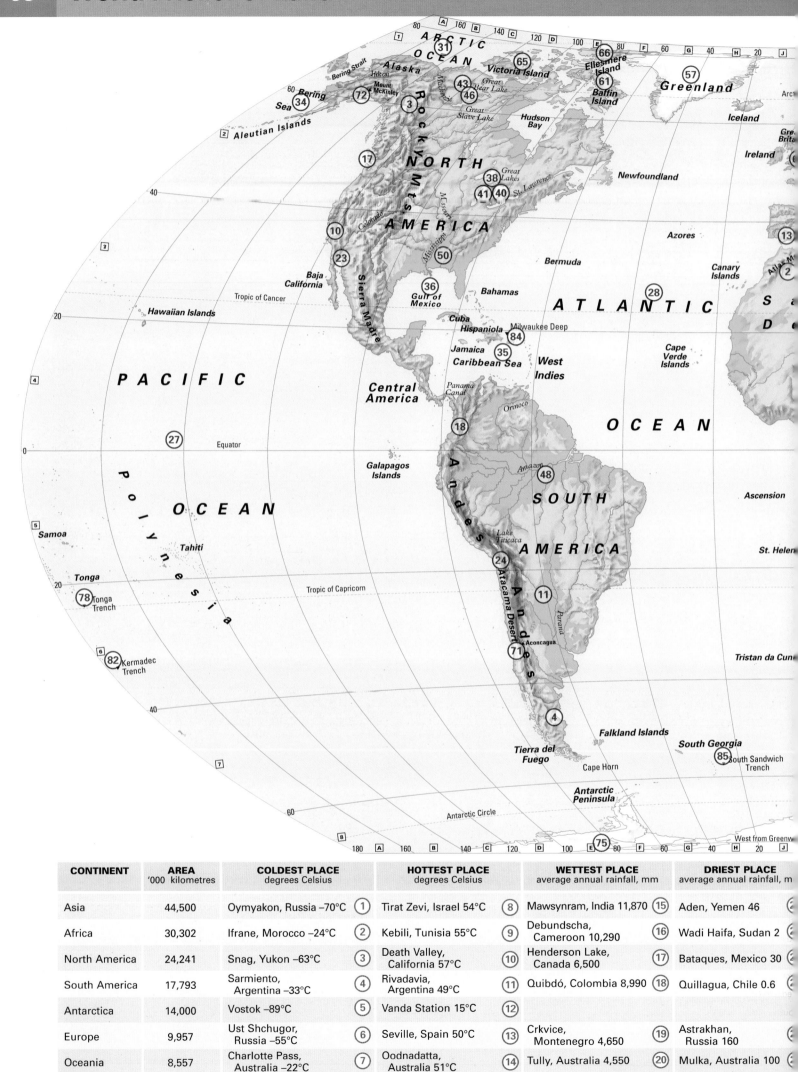

CONTINENT	AREA '000 kilometres	COLDEST PLACE degrees Celsius		HOTTEST PLACE degrees Celsius		WETTEST PLACE average annual rainfall, mm		DRIEST PLACE average annual rainfall, m
Asia	44,500	Oymyakon, Russia −70°C	①	Tirat Zevi, Israel 54°C	⑧	Mawsynram, India 11,870 ⑮		Aden, Yemen 46
Africa	30,302	Ifrane, Morocco −24°C	②	Kebili, Tunisia 55°C	⑨	Debundscha, Cameroon 10,290	⑯	Wadi Haifa, Sudan 2
North America	24,241	Snag, Yukon −63°C	③	Death Valley, California 57°C	⑩	Henderson Lake, Canada 6,500	⑰	Bataques, Mexico 30
South America	17,793	Sarmiento, Argentina −33°C	④	Rivadavia, Argentina 49°C	⑪	Quibdó, Colombia 8,990	⑱	Quillagua, Chile 0.6
Antarctica	14,000	Vostok −89°C	⑤	Vanda Station 15°C	⑫			
Europe	9,957	Ust Shchugor, Russia −55°C	⑥	Seville, Spain 50°C	⑬	Crkvice, Montenegro 4,650	⑲	Astrakhan, Russia 160
Oceania	8,557	Charlotte Pass, Australia −22°C	⑦	Oodnadatta, Australia 51°C	⑭	Tully, Australia 4,550	⑳	Mulka, Australia 100

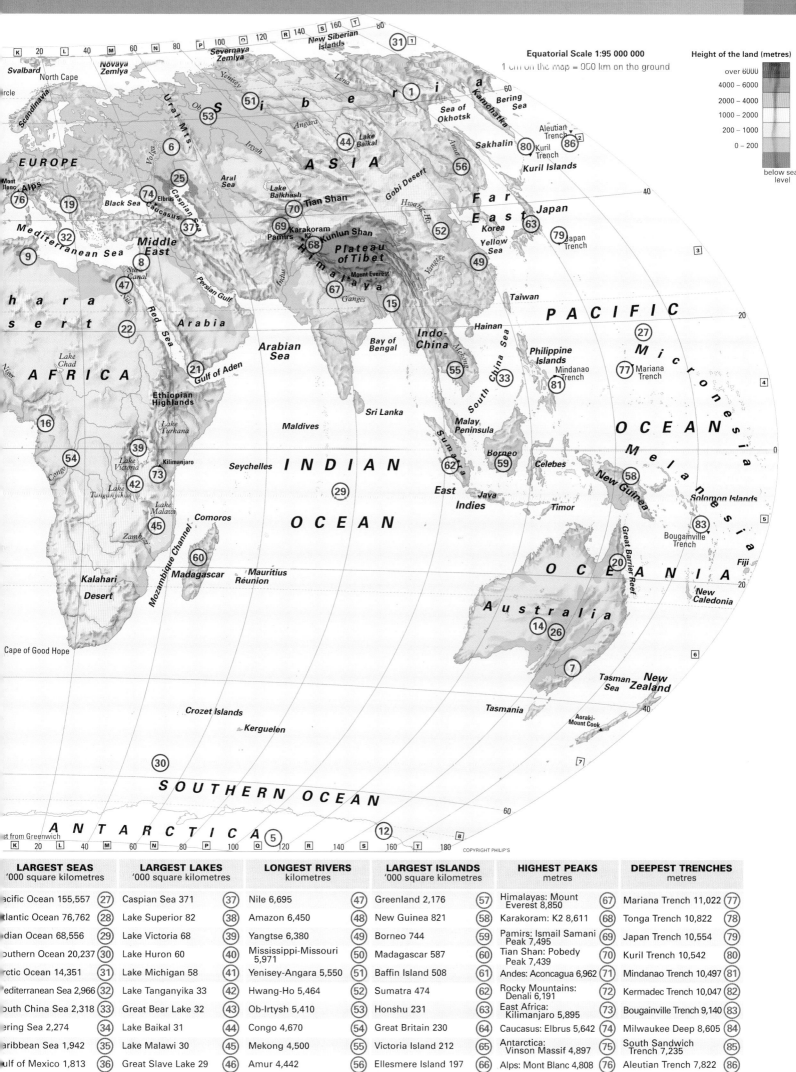

Equatorial Scale 1:95 000 000
1 cm on the map = 950 km on the ground

Height of the land (metres)

over 6000	
4000 – 6000	
2000 – 4000	
1000 – 2000	
200 – 1000	
0 – 200	

below sea level

COPYRIGHT PHILIP'S

LARGEST SEAS '000 square kilometres		LARGEST LAKES '000 square kilometres		LONGEST RIVERS kilometres		LARGEST ISLANDS '000 square kilometres		HIGHEST PEAKS metres		DEEPEST TRENCHES metres	
Pacific Ocean 155,557	(27)	Caspian Sea 371	(37)	Nile 6,695	(47)	Greenland 2,176	(57)	Himalayas: Mount Everest 8,850	(67)	Mariana Trench 11,022	(77)
Atlantic Ocean 76,762	(28)	Lake Superior 82	(38)	Amazon 6,450	(48)	New Guinea 821	(58)	Karakoram: K2 8,611	(68)	Tonga Trench 10,822	(78)
Indian Ocean 68,556	(29)	Lake Victoria 68	(39)	Yangtse 6,380	(49)	Borneo 744	(59)	Pamirs: Ismail Samani Peak 7,495	(69)	Japan Trench 10,554	(79)
Southern Ocean 20,237	(30)	Lake Huron 60	(40)	Mississippi-Missouri 5,971	(50)	Madagascar 587	(60)	Tian Shan: Pobedy Peak 7,439	(70)	Kuril Trench 10,542	(80)
Arctic Ocean 14,351	(31)	Lake Michigan 58	(41)	Yenisey-Angara 5,550	(51)	Baffin Island 508	(61)	Andes: Aconcagua 6,962	(71)	Mindanao Trench 10,497	(81)
Mediterranean Sea 2,966	(32)	Lake Tanganyika 33	(42)	Hwang-Ho 5,464	(52)	Sumatra 474	(62)	Rocky Mountains: Denali 6,191	(72)	Kermadec Trench 10,047	(82)
South China Sea 2,318	(33)	Great Bear Lake 32	(43)	Ob-Irtysh 5,410	(53)	Honshu 231	(63)	East Africa: Kilimanjaro 5,895	(73)	Bougainville Trench 9,140	(83)
Bering Sea 2,274	(34)	Lake Baikal 31	(44)	Congo 4,670	(54)	Great Britain 230	(64)	Caucasus: Elbrus 5,642	(74)	Milwaukee Deep 8,605	(84)
Caribbean Sea 1,942	(35)	Lake Malawi 30	(45)	Mekong 4,500	(55)	Victoria Island 212	(65)	Antarctica: Vinson Massif 4,897	(75)	South Sandwich Trench 7,235	(85)
Gulf of Mexico 1,813	(36)	Great Slave Lake 29	(46)	Amur 4,442	(56)	Ellesmere Island 197	(66)	Alps: Mont Blanc 4,808	(76)	Aleutian Trench 7,822	(86)

ALB. = ALBANIA
B.-H. = BOSNIA-HERZEGOVINA
BELG. = BELGIUM
CR. = CROATIA
CZECH. = CZECH REPUBLIC
EST. = ESTONIA
HUNG. = HUNGARY
K. = KOSOVO
LAT. = LATVIA
LEB. = LEBANON
LITH. = LITHUANIA
LUX. = LUXEMBOURG

COUNTRY	'000 people	COUNTRY	'000 people	COUNTRY	'000 people	COUNTRY	'000 people	COUNTRY	'000 people
China	1,367,485	Mexico	121,737	France	66,554	Ukraine	44,429	Nepal	31,551
India	1,251,696	Philippines	100,998	United Kingdom	64,088	Argentina	43,432	Malaysia	30,514
USA	321,369	Ethiopia	99,466	Italy	61,855	Algeria	39,542	Peru	30,445
Indonesia	255,994	Vietnam	94,349	Burma	56,320	Poland	38,562	Venezuela	29,275
Brazil	204,260	Egypt	88,487	South Africa	53,676	Uganda	37,102	Uzbekistan	29,200
Pakistan	199,086	Iran	81,824	Tanzania	51,046	Iraq	37,056	Saudi Arabia	27,752
Nigeria	181,562	Germany	80,854	South Korea	49,115	Sudan	36,109	Yemen	26,737
Bangladesh	168,958	Turkey	79,414	Spain	48,146	Canada	35,100	Ghana	26,328
Russia	142,424	Congo (Dem. Rep.)	79,375	Colombia	46,737	Morocco	33,323	Mozambique	25,303
Japan	126,920	Thailand	67,976	Kenya	45,925	Afghanistan	32,564	North Korea	24,983

Equatorial Scale 1:95 000 000
1 cm on the map = 950 km on the ground

M. = MONTENEGRO
MACED. = MACEDONIA
MOLD. = MOLDOVA
NETH.= NETHERLANDS
SERB. = SERBIA
SLO. = SLOVENIA
SLOV. = SLOVAK REPUBLIC
SWITZ. = SWITZERLAND
U.A.E. = UNITED ARAB EMIRATES
U.K. = UNITED KINGDOM
U.S.A. = UNITED STATES OF AMERICA

COUNTRY	'000 people	COUNTRY	'000 people	COUNTRY	'000 people	COUNTRY	'000 people	COUNTRY	'000 people
Madagascar	23,813	Niger	18,046	Zimbabwe	14,230	Bolivia	10,801	Azerbaijan	9,781
Cameroon	23,739	Malawi	17,965	Senegal	13,976	Greece	10,776	Belarus	9,590
Taiwan	23,415	Chile	17,508	Rwanda	12,662	Burundi	10,742	Honduras	8,747
Ivory Coast	23,295	Syria	17,065	South Sudan	12,043	Czech Republic	10,645	Austria	8,666
Australia	22,751	Mali	16,956	Guinea	11,780	Somalia	10,616	Tajikistan	8,192
Sri Lanka	22,053	Netherlands	16,948	Chad	11,631	Dominican Republic	10,479	Switzerland	8,122
Romania	21,666	Ecuador	15,868	Belgium	11,324	Benin	10,449	Jordan	8,118
Angola	19,625	Cambodia	15,709	Tunisia	11,037	Haiti	10,110	Israel	8,049
Burkina Faso	18,932	Zambia	15,066	Cuba	11,031	Hungary	9,898	Togo	7,552
Kazakhstan	18,157	Guatemala	14,919	Portugal	10,825	Sweden	9,802	Bulgaria	7,187

COPYRIGHT PHILIP'S

CLIMATE REGIONS

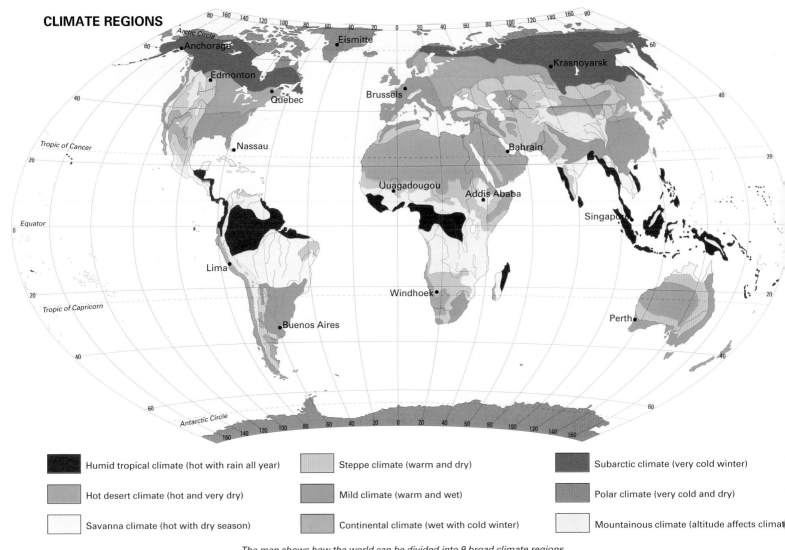

Humid tropical climate (hot with rain all year)

Hot desert climate (hot and very dry)

Savanna climate (hot with dry season)

Steppe climate (warm and dry)

Mild climate (warm and wet)

Continental climate (wet with cold winter)

Subarctic climate (very cold winter)

Polar climate (very cold and dry)

Mountainous climate (altitude affects climat

The map shows how the world can be divided into 9 broad climate regions.

CLIMATE GRAPHS

The graphs below give examples of places within each climate region, showing how temperature and rainfall vary from month to month.

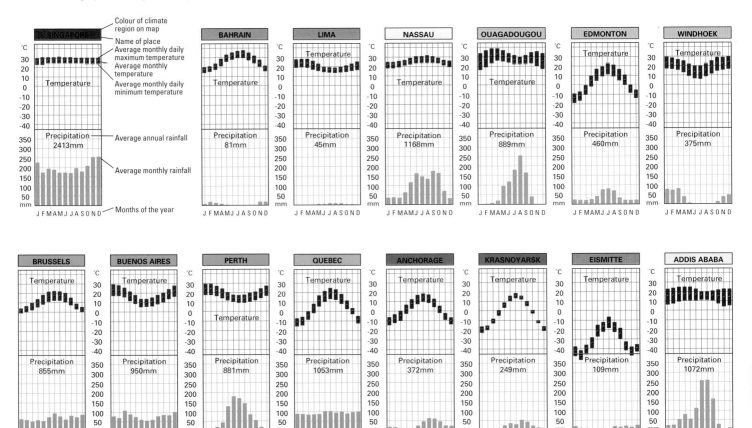

HUMID TROPICAL CLIMATE

HOT DESERT CLIMATE

SAVANNA

MILD CLIMATE

POLAR CLIMATE

MOUNTAINOUS CLIMATE

ANNUAL RAINFALL

Mawsynram, India
Over 11,800 mm
has fallen in a year
Wettest place
on Earth

Atacama Desert
Driest place on Earth
No rain has ever
been recorded

Average annual
rainfall

3000 mm
2000 mm
1000 mm
500 mm
250 mm

Tropic of Cancer

Equator

Tropic of Capricorn

JANUARY TEMPERATURE

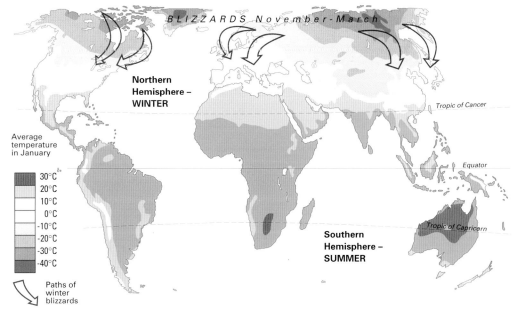

BLIZZARDS November–March

Northern
Hemisphere –
WINTER

Southern
Hemisphere –
SUMMER

Average
temperature
in January

30°C
20°C
10°C
0°C
-10°C
-20°C
-30°C
-40°C

Paths of
winter
blizzards

Tropic of Cancer

Equator

Tropic of Capricorn

JULY TEMPERATURE

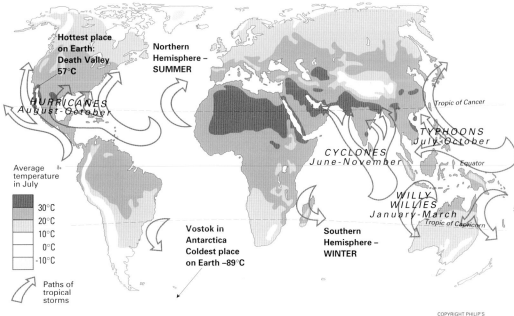

Hottest place
on Earth:
Death Valley
57°C

Northern
Hemisphere –
SUMMER

HURRICANES August–October

TYPHOONS July–October

CYCLONES June–November

WILLY WILLIES January–March

Vostok in
Antarctica
Coldest place
on Earth –89°C

Southern
Hemisphere –
WINTER

Average
temperature
in July

30°C
20°C
10°C
0°C
-10°C

Paths of
tropical
storms

Tropic of Cancer

Equator

Tropic of Capricorn

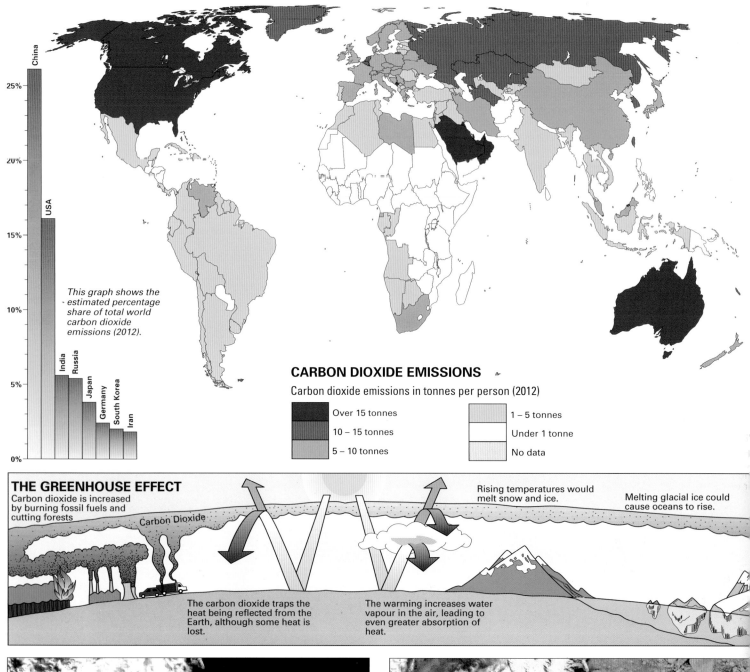

This graph shows the estimated percentage share of total world carbon dioxide emissions (2012).

CARBON DIOXIDE EMISSIONS

Carbon dioxide emissions in tonnes per person (2012)

- Over 15 tonnes
- 10 – 15 tonnes
- 5 – 10 tonnes
- 1 – 5 tonnes
- Under 1 tonne
- No data

THE GREENHOUSE EFFECT

Carbon dioxide is increased by burning fossil fuels and cutting forests

Carbon Dioxide

The carbon dioxide traps the heat being reflected from the Earth, although some heat is lost.

The warming increases water vapour in the air, leading to even greater absorption of heat.

Rising temperatures would melt snow and ice.

Melting glacial ice could cause oceans to rise.

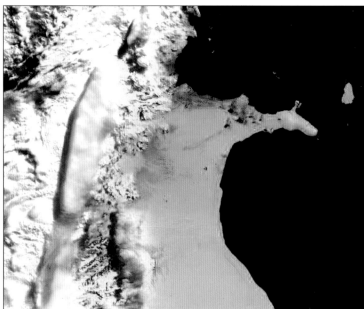

▲ **Larsen B ice shelf, Antarctica.** Between January and March 2002, Larsen B ice shelf on the Antarctic Peninsula collapsed. The image on the left shows its area before the collapse, while the image on the right shows the area after the collapse. The 200 m thick ice sheet had been retreating before this date, but over 500 billion tonnes of ice collapsed in under a month. This was due to rising temperatures of 0.5°C per year in this part of Antarctica. Satellite images like these are the only way for scientists to monitor inaccessible areas of the world.

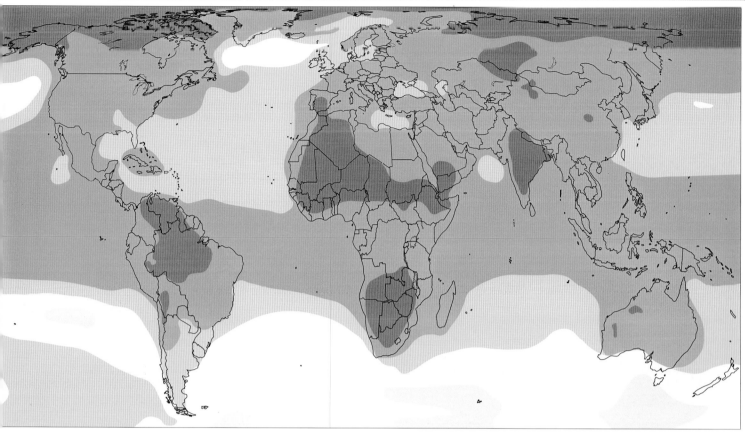

PREDICTED CHANGE IN TEMPERATURE

The difference between actual annual average surface air temperature, 1969–1990, and predicted annual average surface air temperature, 2070–2100

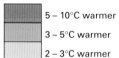
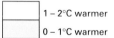

5 – 10°C warmer	1 – 2°C warmer
3 – 5°C warmer	0 – 1°C warmer
2 – 3°C warmer	

These maps shows the predicted increase assuming a 'medium growth' of the global economy and assuming that no measures to combat the emission of greenhouse gases are taken.

It should be noted that these predicted annual average changes mask quite significant seasonal detail.

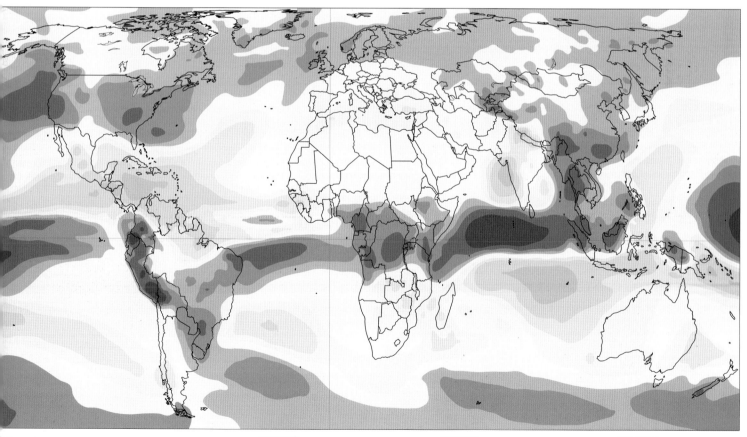

PREDICTED CHANGE IN RAINFALL

The difference between actual annual average rainfall, 1969–1990, and predicted annual average rainfall, 2070–2100

Over 2 mm more rain per day	0.2 – 0.5 mm more rain per day	0.5 – 1 mm less rain per day
1 – 2 mm more rain per day	No change	1 – 2 mm less rain per day
Over 2 mm more rain per day	0.2 – 0.5 mm less rain per day	Over 2 mm less rain per day

Source: The Hadley Centre of Climate Prediction and Research, Met Office

TUNDRA AND MOUNTAIN VEGETATION

NEEDLELEAF EVERGREEN FOREST

MID-LATITUDE GRASSLAND

TROPICAL BROADLEAF RAINFOREST

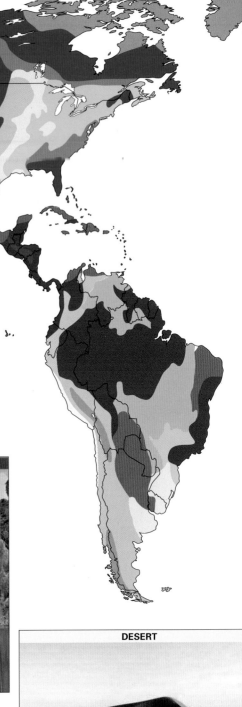

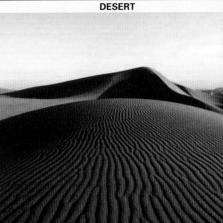

DESERT

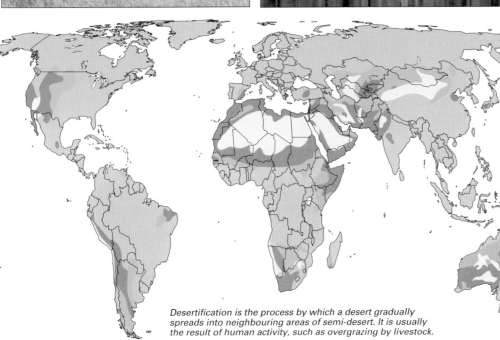

Desertification is the process by which a desert gradually spreads into neighbouring areas of semi-desert. It is usually the result of human activity, such as overgrazing by livestock.

DESERTIFICATION

Existing desert

Areas with a high risk of desertification

Areas with a moderate risk of desertification

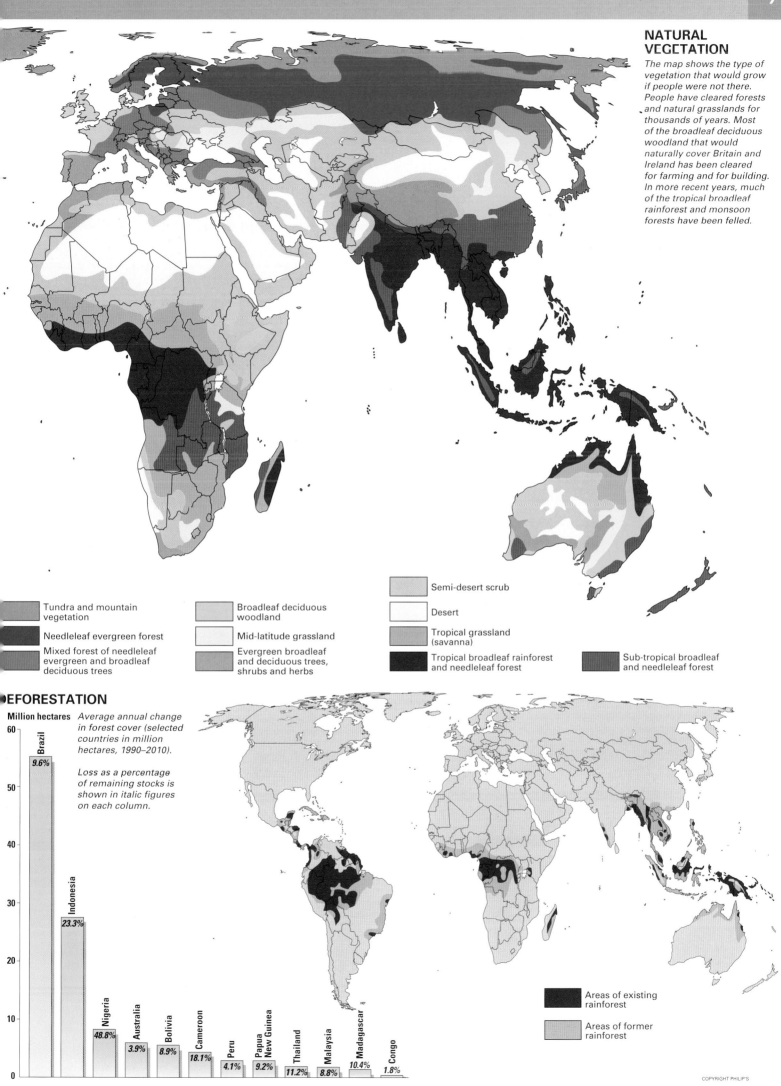

NATURAL VEGETATION

The map shows the type of vegetation that would grow if people were not there. People have cleared forests and natural grasslands for thousands of years. Most of the broadleaf deciduous woodland that would naturally cover Britain and Ireland has been cleared for farming and for building. In more recent years, much of the tropical broadleaf rainforest and monsoon forests have been felled.

Tundra and mountain vegetation

Needleleaf evergreen forest

Mixed forest of needleleaf evergreen and broadleaf deciduous trees

Broadleaf deciduous woodland

Mid-latitude grassland

Evergreen broadleaf and deciduous trees, shrubs and herbs

Semi-desert scrub

Desert

Tropical grassland (savanna)

Tropical broadleaf rainforest and needleleaf forest

Sub-tropical broadleaf and needleleaf forest

DEFORESTATION

Million hectares *Average annual change in forest cover (selected countries in million hectares, 1990–2010).*

Loss as a percentage of remaining stocks is shown in italic figures on each column.

Brazil *9.6%*
Indonesia *23.3%*
Nigeria *48.8%*
Australia *3.9%*
Bolivia *8.9%*
Cameroon *18.1%*
Peru *4.1%*
Papua New Guinea *9.2%*
Thailand *11.2%*
Malaysia *8.8%*
Madagascar *10.4%*
Congo *1.8%*

Areas of existing rainforest

Areas of former rainforest

COPYRIGHT PHILIP'S

CONTINENTAL DRIFT

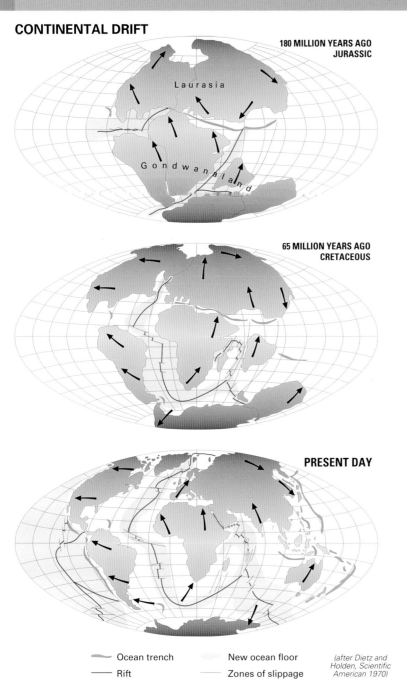

180 MILLION YEARS AGO JURASSIC

65 MILLION YEARS AGO CRETACEOUS

PRESENT DAY

(after Dietz and Holden, Scientific American 1970)

〜 Ocean trench

— Rift

New ocean floor

Zones of slippage

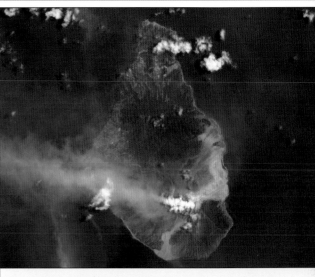

▲ In 1995, after almost 400 years lying dormant, the Soufrière Hills volcano on the Caribbean island of Montserrat began a series of eruptions. Further eruptions in 1996 and 1997 left the south of the island uninhabitable and 5,000 people had to be evacuated to the northern zone. Steam can be seen rising from the volcano in the false colour satellite image, above.

SOUFRIÈRE HILLS VOLCANO, MONTSERRAT

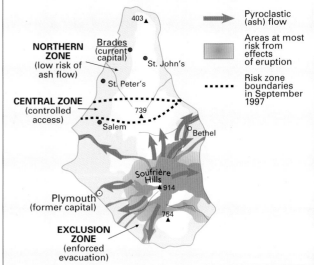

NORTHERN ZONE (low risk of ash flow)

Brades (current capital)

St. John's

St. Peter's

CENTRAL ZONE (controlled access)

Salem

Bethel

739

403

EXCLUSION ZONE (enforced evacuation)

Plymouth (former capital)

Soufrière Hills ▲914

754

→ Pyroclastic (ash) flow

Areas at most risk from effects of eruption

∙∙∙∙ Risk zone boundaries in September 1997

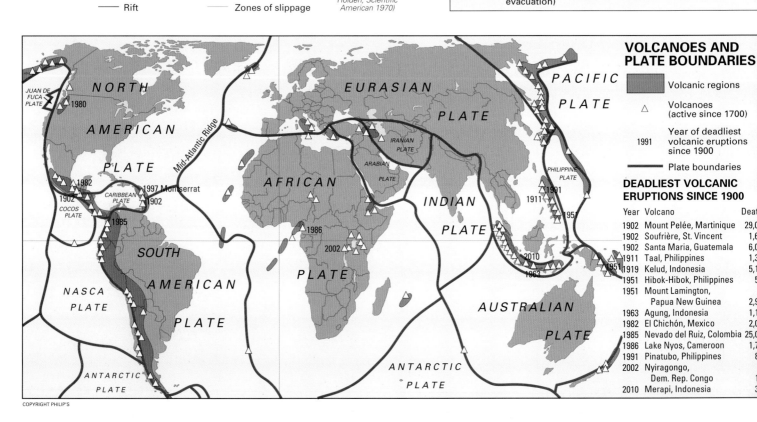

VOLCANOES AND PLATE BOUNDARIES

Volcanic regions

△ Volcanoes (active since 1700)

1991 Year of deadliest volcanic eruptions since 1900

— Plate boundaries

DEADLIEST VOLCANIC ERUPTIONS SINCE 1900

Year	Volcano	Deaths
1902	Mount Pelée, Martinique	29,025
1902	Soufrière, St. Vincent	1,680
1902	Santa Maria, Guatemala	6,000
1911	Taal, Philippines	1,335
1919	Kelud, Indonesia	5,110
1951	Hibok-Hibok, Philippines	500
1951	Mount Lamington, Papua New Guinea	2,942
1963	Agung, Indonesia	1,184
1982	El Chichón, Mexico	2,000
1985	Nevado del Ruiz, Colombia	25,000
1986	Lake Nyos, Cameroon	1,700
1991	Pinatubo, Philippines	800
2002	Nyiragongo, Dem. Rep. Congo	147
2010	Merapi, Indonesia	353

COPYRIGHT PHILIP'S

PLATE TECTONICS IN THE CARIBBEAN

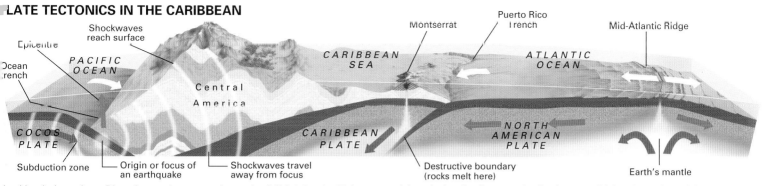

The North American Plate is moving away from the Mid-Atlantic Ridge and towards the Caribbean Plate at a rate of 30-40mm a year. The edge of the North American Plate is forced downwards under the Caribbean Plate. As the North American Plate descends, the rocks melt and are destroyed. This is called a *destructive boundary*. The destructive boundary to the east of the Caribbean has caused the Puerto Rico Trench and the chain of volcanoes in the Leeward Islands such as Montserrat. The molten rocks along the destructive boundary are forced upwards through cracks at the edge of the Caribbean Plate to pour out as lava from volcanoes. Earthquakes are also common along destructive plate boundaries, as is the case in Central America, along the boundary between the Caribbean and Cocos Plates.

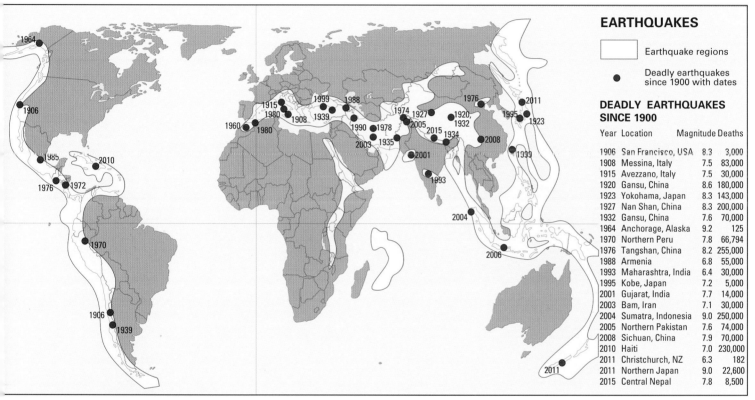

EARTHQUAKES

▢ Earthquake regions

● Deadly earthquakes since 1900 with dates

DEADLY EARTHQUAKES SINCE 1900

Year	Location	Magnitude	Deaths
1906	San Francisco, USA	8.3	3,000
1908	Messina, Italy	7.5	83,000
1915	Avezzano, Italy	7.5	30,000
1920	Gansu, China	8.6	180,000
1923	Yokohama, Japan	8.3	143,000
1927	Nan Shan, China	8.3	200,000
1932	Gansu, China	7.6	70,000
1964	Anchorage, Alaska	9.2	125
1970	Northern Peru	7.8	66,794
1976	Tangshan, China	8.2	255,000
1988	Armenia	6.8	55,000
1993	Maharashtra, India	6.4	30,000
1995	Kobe, Japan	7.2	5,000
2001	Gujarat, India	7.7	14,000
2003	Bam, Iran	7.1	30,000
2004	Sumatra, Indonesia	9.0	250,000
2005	Northern Pakistan	7.6	74,000
2008	Sichuan, China	7.9	70,000
2010	Haiti	7.0	230,000
2011	Christchurch, NZ	6.3	182
2011	Northern Japan	9.0	22,600
2015	Central Nepal	7.8	8,500

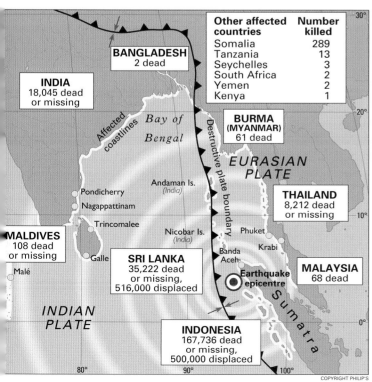

Other affected countries	Number killed
Somalia	289
Tanzania	13
Seychelles	3
South Africa	2
Yemen	2
Kenya	1

INDIAN OCEAN TSUNAMI

On 26 December 2004, an earthquake off the coast of Sumatra triggered a deadly tsunami that swept across the Indian Ocean, causing devastation in many countries (see map left).
The image below shows the turbulent receding waters of the tsunami, on the west coast of Sri Lanka. Such imagery enabled rescuers to assess the worst affected areas.

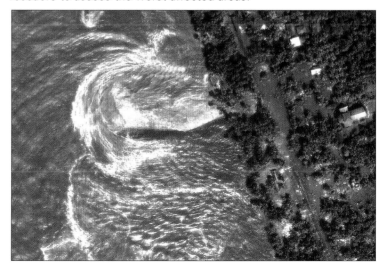

POPULATION DENSITY BY COUNTRY

Density of people per square kilometre (2015)

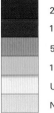

- 250 per km² and over
- 100 – 250 per km²
- 50 – 100 per km²
- 10 – 50 per km²
- Under 10 per km²
- No data

Most and least densely populated countries

Most per km²		Least per km²	
Monaco	30,535	Mongolia	2
Singapore	8,345	Namibia	3
Bahrain	1,952	Australia	3
Malta	1,294	Iceland	3
Maldives	1,311	Guyana	3

UK 265 per km²

POPULATION CHANGE

Expected change in total population (2004–2050)

- Over 125% gain
- 100 – 125% gain
- 50 – 100% gain
- 25 – 50% gain
- 0 – 25% gain
- No change or loss

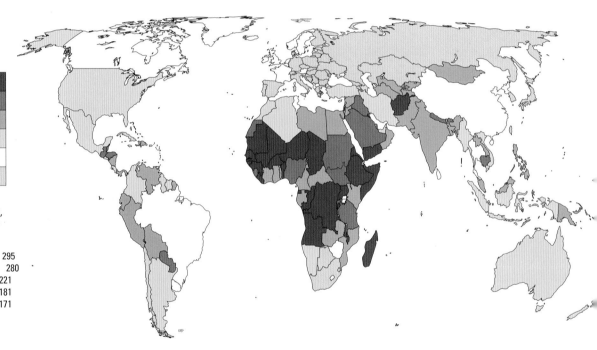

Based on estimates for the year 2050, the ten most populous nations in the world will be, in millions:

India	1,628	Pakistan	295
China	1,437	Bangladesh	280
USA	420	Brazil	221
Indonesia	308	Congo Dem. Rep.	181
Nigeria	307	Ethiopia	171

UK (2050) 77 million

URBAN POPULATION

Percentage of total population living in towns and cities (2015)

- 80% urban and over
- 60 – 80% urban
- 40 – 60% urban
- 20 – 40% urban
- Under 20% urban
- No data

Countries that are the most and least urbanized (%)

Most urbanized		Least urbanized	
Monaco	100	Trinidad & Tobago	8
Nauru	100	Burundi	12
Singapore	100	Papua N. Guinea	13

UK 83% urban

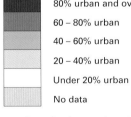

In 2008, for the first time in history, more than half the world's population lived in urban areas.

POPULATION BY CONTINENT

In this diagram the size of each continent is in proportion to its population (2015).

Each square represents 10 million people.

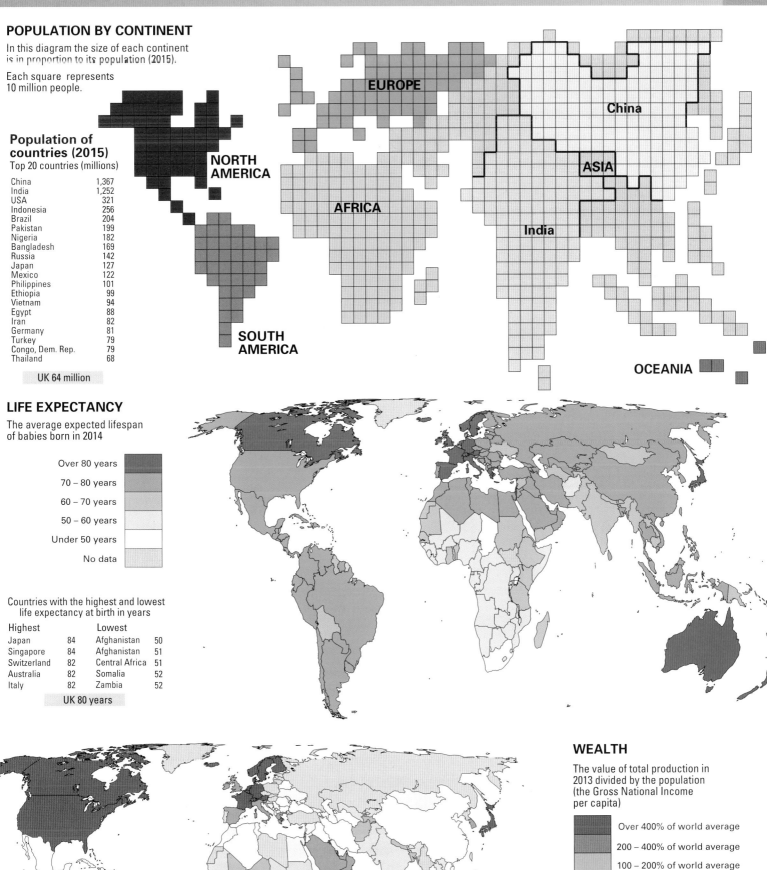

Population of countries (2015)
Top 20 countries (millions)

China	1,367
India	1,252
USA	321
Indonesia	256
Brazil	204
Pakistan	199
Nigeria	182
Bangladesh	169
Russia	142
Japan	127
Mexico	122
Philippines	101
Ethiopia	99
Vietnam	94
Egypt	88
Iran	82
Germany	81
Turkey	79
Congo, Dem. Rep.	79
Thailand	68

UK 64 million

LIFE EXPECTANCY

The average expected lifespan of babies born in 2014

- Over 80 years
- 70 – 80 years
- 60 – 70 years
- 50 – 60 years
- Under 50 years
- No data

Countries with the highest and lowest life expectancy at birth in years

Highest		Lowest	
Japan	84	Afghanistan	50
Singapore	84	Afghanistan	51
Switzerland	82	Central Africa	51
Australia	82	Somalia	52
Italy	82	Zambia	52

UK 80 years

WEALTH

The value of total production in 2013 divided by the population (the Gross National Income per capita)

- Over 400% of world average
- 200 – 400% of world average
- 100 – 200% of world average

World average wealth per person $9,135

- 50 – 100% of world average
- 25 – 50% of world average
- 10 – 25% of world average
- Under 10% of world average
- No data

Top 3 countries		Bottom 3 countries	
Norway	$102,610	Malawi	$270
Qatar	$85,550	Burundi	$280
Switzerland	$80,950	Central Africa	$320

UK $39,110

COPYRIGHT PHILIP'S

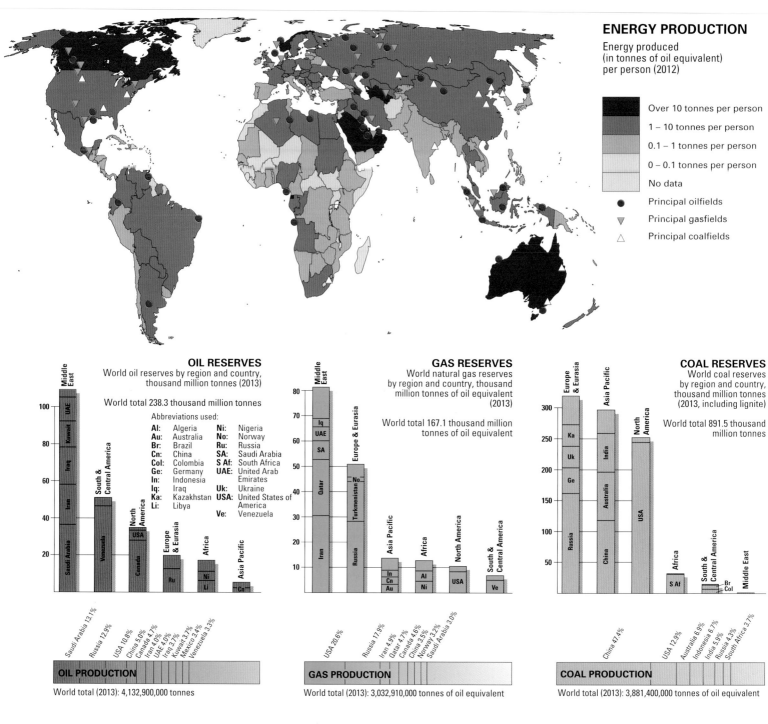

ENERGY PRODUCTION

Energy produced
(in tonnes of oil equivalent)
per person (2012)

- Over 10 tonnes per person
- 1 – 10 tonnes per person
- 0.1 – 1 tonnes per person
- 0 – 0.1 tonnes per person
- No data
- ● Principal oilfields
- ▼ Principal gasfields
- △ Principal coalfields

OIL RESERVES

World oil reserves by region and country,
thousand million tonnes (2013)

World total 238.3 thousand million tonnes

Abbreviations used:

Al:	Algeria	**Ni:**	Nigeria
Au:	Australia	**No:**	Norway
Br:	Brazil	**Ru:**	Russia
Cn:	China	**SA:**	Saudi Arabia
Col:	Colombia	**S Af:**	South Africa
Ge:	Germany	**UAE:**	United Arab
In:	Indonesia		Emirates
Iq:	Iraq	**Uk:**	Ukraine
Ka:	Kazakhstan	**USA:**	United States of
Li:	Libya		America
		Ve:	Venezuela

OIL PRODUCTION
Saudi Arabia 13.1% Russia 12.9% USA 10.8% China 5.0% Canada 4.7% Iran 4.0% UAE 4.0% Iraq 3.7% Kuwait 3.7% Mexico 3.4% Venezuela 3.3%

World total (2013): 4,132,900,000 tonnes

GAS RESERVES

World natural gas reserves
by region and country, thousand
million tonnes of oil equivalent
(2013)

World total 167.1 thousand million
tonnes of oil equivalent

GAS PRODUCTION
USA 20.6% Russia 17.9% Iran 4.9% Qatar 4.7% Canada 4.6% China 3.5% Norway 3.2% Saudi Arabia 3.0%

World total (2013): 3,032,910,000 tonnes of oil equivalent

COAL RESERVES

World coal reserves
by region and country,
thousand million tonnes
(2013, including lignite)

World total 891.5 thousand
million tonnes

COAL PRODUCTION
China 47.4% USA 12.9% Australia 6.9% Indonesia 6.7% India 5.6% Russia 4.3% South Africa 3.7%

World total (2013): 3,881,400,000 tonnes of oil equivalent

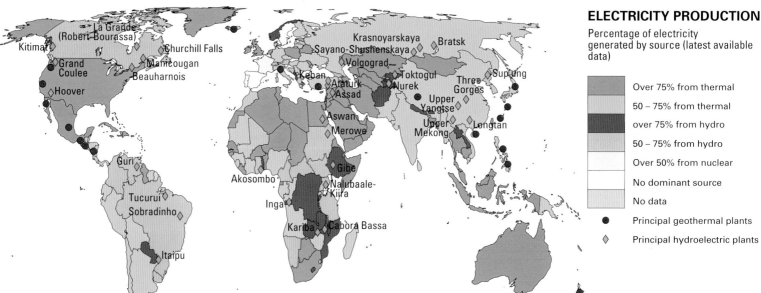

ELECTRICITY PRODUCTION

Percentage of electricity
generated by source (latest available
data)

- Over 75% from thermal
- 50 – 75% from thermal
- over 75% from hydro
- 50 – 75% from hydro
- Over 50% from nuclear
- No dominant source
- No data
- ● Principal geothermal plants
- ◇ Principal hydroelectric plants

FOOD PRODUCTION

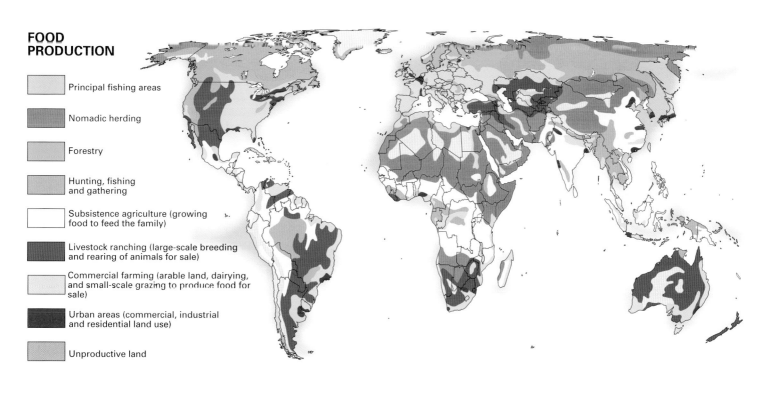

- Principal fishing areas
- Nomadic herding
- Forestry
- Hunting, fishing and gathering
- Subsistence agriculture (growing food to feed the family)
- Livestock ranching (large-scale breeding and rearing of animals for sale)
- Commercial farming (arable land, dairying, and small-scale grazing to produce food for sale)
- Urban areas (commercial, industrial and residential land use)
- Unproductive land

DAILY FOOD CONSUMPTION

Average daily food intake in calories per person (2014)

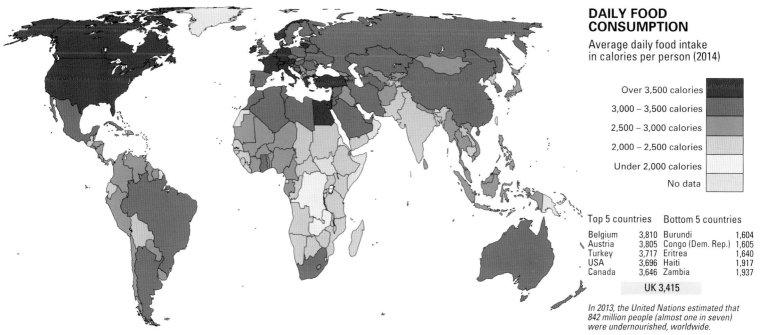

- Over 3,500 calories
- 3,000 – 3,500 calories
- 2,500 – 3,000 calories
- 2,000 – 2,500 calories
- Under 2,000 calories
- No data

Top 5 countries		Bottom 5 countries	
Belgium	3,810	Burundi	1,604
Austria	3,805	Congo (Dem. Rep.)	1,605
Turkey	3,717	Eritrea	1,640
USA	3,696	Haiti	1,917
Canada	3,646	Zambia	1,937

UK 3,415

In 2013, the United Nations estimated that 842 million people (almost one in seven) were undernourished, worldwide.

WATER SUPPLY

The percentage of total population with access to safe drinking water (2015)

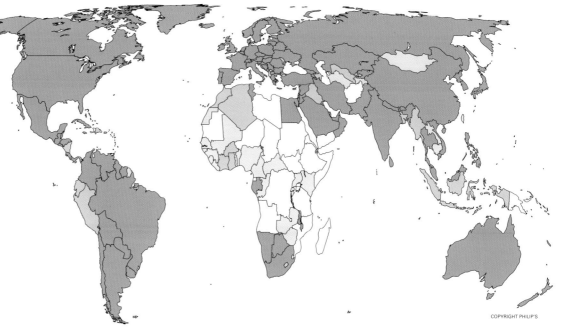

- Over 90% with safe water
- 80 – 90% with safe water
- 60 – 80% with safe water
- Under 60% with safe water
- No data

Least well-provided countries

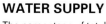

Somalia	32%
Papua New Guinea	40%
Equatorial Guinea	48%
Angola	49%
Chad	51%
Mozambique	51%

One person in eight in the world has no access to a safe water supply.

COPYRIGHT PHILIP'S

WORLD TRADE

The percentage share of total world exports by value (2013)

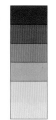

Over 10%

1.0 – 10%

0.1 – 1.0%

0 – 0.1%

0%

No data

 Member of 'G8'

The members of 'G8' account for more than half the total trade. The majority of nations contribute less than one quarter of 1% to the worldwide total of exports; EU countries account for over 30%; the Pacific Rim nations over 45%.

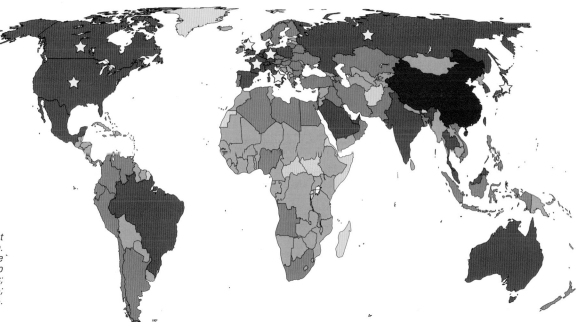

GLOBALIZATION INDEX

Index of globalization (2015)

Over 80

60 – 80

40 – 60

20 – 40

No data

The index is a measure of economic, political and social globalization. The higher values show a greater level of globalization.

INTERNATIONAL AID

Official Development Assistance (ODA) provided and received, US$ per person (2012)

Over $250

$100 – $250

Under $100 — PROVIDERS

Under $10 — RECEIVERS

$10 – $50

$50 – $100

Over $100

No data

Top 5 providers		Top 5 receivers	
Norway	$1,010	Tuvalu	$2,484
Luxembourg	$784	Marshall Is	$1,446
Malta	$784	Micronesia	$1,113
Sweden	$576	Tonga	$746
Denmark	$486	Palau	$723

UK provides $220

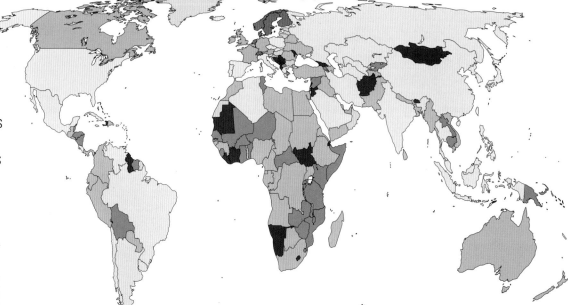

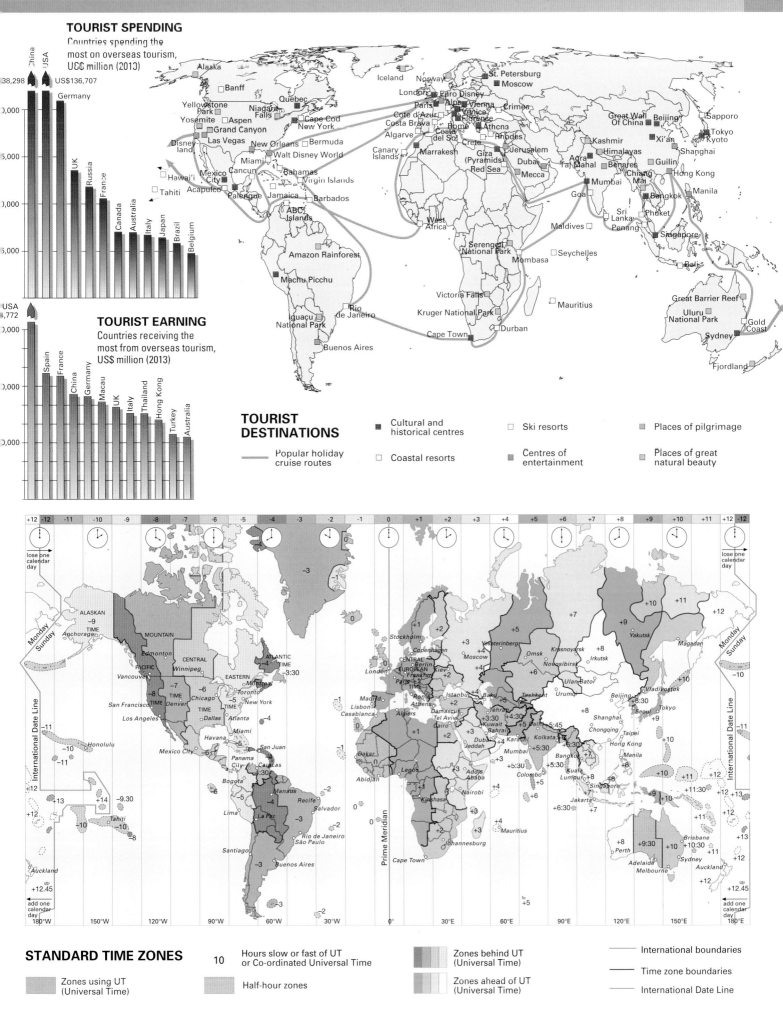

The Earth rotates through 360° in 24 hours, and so moves 15° every hour. The World is divided into 24 standard time zones, each centred on lines of longitude at 15° intervals. The Greenwich Meridian (or Prime Meridian) lies on the centre of the first zone. All places to the west of Greenwich are one hour behind for every 15° of longitude; places to the east are ahead by one hour for every 15°.

FLAG	COUNTRY	CAPITAL CITY	AREA thousand square kilometres 2015	POPULATION in millions 2015	POPULATION CHANGE percent per year 2015	BIRTHS per thousand people 2015	DEATHS per thousand people 2015	LIFE EXPECTANCY years 2015	INCOME US $ per person 2014
	Afghanistan	Kabul	652	32.6	2.3	39	14	51	2,000
	Albania	Tirane	28.7	3.0	0.3	13	7	78	10,300
	Algeria	Algiers	2,382	39.5	1.8	24	4	77	13,900
	Angola	Luanda	1,247	19.6	2.8	39	11	56	6,500
	Argentina	Buenos Aires	2,780	43.4	0.9	17	7	78	7,600
	Armenia	Yerevan	29.8	3.1	-0.1	14	9	74	8,500
	Australia	Canberra	7,741	22.8	1.1	12	7	82	42,900
	Austria	Vienna	83.9	8.7	0.6	9	9	81	45,000
	Azerbaijan	Baku	86.6	9.8	1.0	17	7	72	16,900
	Bahamas	Nassau	13.9	0.3	0.9	16	7	72	22,300
	Bahrain	Manama	0.7	1.3	2.4	14	3	79	37,700
	Bangladesh	Dhaka	144	169.0	1.6	21	6	71	3,300
	Barbados	Bridgetown	0.4	0.3	0.3	12	8	75	14,800
	Belarus	Minsk	208	9.6	-0.2	11	13	72	17,600
	Belgium	Brussels	30.5	11.3	0.8	11	10	81	43,000
	Belize	Belmopan	23.0	0.3	1.9	25	6	69	7,600
	Benin	Porto-Novo	113	10.4	2.8	36	8	61	1,900
	Bhutan	Thimphu	47.0	0.7	1.1	18	7	70	7,600
	Bolivia	La Paz/Sucre	1,099	10.8	1.6	23	7	69	6,300
	Bosnia-Herzegovina	Sarajevo	51.2	3.9	-0.1	9	10	77	10,000
	Botswana	Gaborone	582	2.2	1.2	21	13	54	16,000
	Brazil	Brasília	8,514	204.3	0.8	14	7	74	15,600
	Brunei	Bandar Seri Begawan	5.8	0.4	1.6	17	4	77	72,200
	Bulgaria	Sofia	111	7.2	-0.6	9	14	74	15,900
	Burkina Faso	Ouagadougou	274	18.9	3.0	42	12	55	1,700
	Burma	Rangoon/Naypyidaw	677	56.3	1.0	18	8	66	200
	Burundi	Bujumbura	27.8	10.7	3.3	42	9	60	800
	Cabo Verde	Praia	4.0	0.5	1.4	20	6	72	6,200
	Cambodia	Phnom Penh	181	15.7	1.6	24	8	64	3,100
	Cameroon	Yaoundé	475	23.7	2.6	36	10	58	2,900
	Canada	Ottawa	9,971	35.1	0.8	10	8	82	43,400
	Central African Republic	Bangui	623	5.4	2.1	35	14	52	600
	Chad	N'djamena	1,284	11.6	1.9	37	14	50	2,100
	Chile	Santiago	757	17.5	0.8	14	6	79	21,600
	China	Beijing	9,597	1,367.5	0.5	12	8	75	13,100
	Colombia	Bogotá	1,139	46.7	1.0	16	5	75	12,900
	Congo	Brazzaville	342	4.8	2.0	36	10	59	5,200
	Congo (Dem. Rep.)	Kinshasa	2,345	79.4	2.5	35	10	57	700
	Costa Rica	San José	51.1	4.8	1.2	16	5	78	14,400
	Croatia	Zagreb	56.5	4.5	-0.1	9	12	77	20,600
	Cuba	Havana	111	11.0	-0.1	10	8	78	18,600
	Cyprus	Nicosia	9.3	1.2	1.4	11	7	79	29,800
	Czech Republic	Prague	78.9	10.6	0.2	10	10	78	27,000

FLAG	COUNTRY	CAPITAL CITY	AREA thousand square kilometres 2015	POPULATION in millions 2015	POPULATION CHANGE percent per year 2015	BIRTHS per thousand people 2015	DEATHS per thousand people 2015	LIFE EXPECTANCY years 2015	INCOME US $ per person 2014
	Denmark	Copenhagen	43.1	5.6	0.2	10	10	79	46,200
	Djibouti	Djibouti	23.2	0.8	2.2	24	8	63	2,600
	Dominican Republic	Santo Domingo	48.5	10.5	1.2	19	5	78	12,600
	East Timor	Dili	14.9	1.2	2.4	34	6	68	5,700
	Ecuador	Quito	284	15.9	1.4	19	5	77	11,200
	Egypt	Cairo	1,001	88.5	1.8	23	5	74	10,300
	El Salvador	San Salvador	21.0	6.1	0.3	16	6	74	8,100
	Equatorial Guinea	Malabo	28.1	0.7	2.5	33	8	64	21,300
	Eritrea	Asmara	118	6.5	2.3	30	8	64	1,500
	Estonia	Tallinn	45.1	1.3	-0.5	11	12	76	25,700
	Ethiopia	Addis Ababa	1,104	99.5	2.9	37	8	61	1,500
	Fiji	Suva	18.3	0.9	0.7	19	6	72	8,000
	Finland	Helsinki	338	5.5	0.4	11	10	81	40,000
	France	Paris	552	66.6	0.4	12	9	82	39,700
	Gabon	Libreville	268	1.7	1.9	34	13	52	16,700
	Gambia	Banjul	11.3	2.0	2.2	31	7	65	1,600
	Georgia	Tbilisi	69.7	4.9	-0.1	13	11	76	7,500
	Germany	Berlin	357	80.9	-0.2	8	11	81	46,800
	Ghana	Accra	239	26.3	2.2	31	7	66	3,900
	Greece	Athens	132	10.8	0.0	9	11	80	26,100
	Guatemala	Guatemala	109	14.9	1.8	25	5	72	7,200
	Guinea	Conakry	246	11.8	2.6	36	9	60	1,100
	Guinea-Bissau	Bissau	36.1	1.7	1.9	33	14	50	1,400
	Guyana	Georgetown	215	0.7	0.0	16	7	68	7,300
	Haiti	Port-au-Prince	27.8	10.1	1.2	22	8	64	1,700
	Honduras	Tegucigalpa	112	8.7	1.7	23	5	71	4,300
	Hungary	Budapest	93.0	9.9	-0.2	9	13	76	23,800
	Iceland	Reykjavik	103	0.3	1.2	14	6	83	42,500
	India	New Delhi	3,287	1,251.7	1.2	20	7	68	5,600
	Indonesia	Jakarta	1,905	256.0	0.9	17	6	72	10,200
	Iran	Tehrān	1,648	81.8	1.2	18	6	71	16,100
	Iraq	Baghdād	438	37.1	2.9	31	4	75	14,400
	Ireland	Dublin	70.3	4.9	1.3	15	6	81	40,800
	Israel	Jerusalem	20.6	8.0	1.6	18	5	82	32,600
	Italy	Rome	301	61.9	0.3	9	10	82	34,700
	Ivory Coast	Yamoussoukro	322	23.3	1.9	29	10	58	3,200
	Jamaica	Kingston	11.0	3.0	0.7	18	7	74	8,500
	Japan	Tokyo	378	126.9	-0.2	8	10	85	37,900
	Jordan	Amman	89.3	8.1	0.8	25	4	74	11,900
	Kazakhstan	Astana	2,725	18.2	1.1	19	8	71	21,600
	Kenya	Nairobi	580	45.9	1.9	26	7	64	2,900
	Korea, North	P'yŏngyang	121	25.0	0.5	15	9	70	1,800
	Korea, South	Seoul	99.3	49.1	0.1	8	7	80	34,600

FLAG	COUNTRY	CAPITAL CITY	AREA thousand square kilometres 2015	POPULATION in millions 2015	POPULATION CHANGE percent per year 2015	BIRTHS per thousand people 2012	DEATHS per thousand people 2015	LIFE EXPECTANCY years 2015	INCOME US $ per person 2014
	Kosovo	Priština	10.9	1.9	-	-	-	75	6,500
	Kuwait	Kuwait	17.8	2.8	1.6	20	2	78	82,200
	Kyrgyzstan	Bishkek	200	5.7	1.1	23	7	70	3,200
	Laos	Vientiane	237	6.9	1.6	24	8	64	5,100
	Latvia	Riga	64.6	2.0	-1.1	10	14	74	23,200
	Lebanon	Beirut	10.4	6.2	0.9	15	5	77	17,200
	Lesotho	Maseru	30.4	1.9	0.3	25	15	53	3,200
	Liberia	Monrovia	111	4.2	2.5	34	10	59	700
	Libya	Tripoli	1,760	6.4	2.2	18	4	76	16,200
	Lithuania	Vilnius	65.2	2.9	-1.0	10	14	75	25,400
	Luxembourg	Luxembourg	2.6	0.6	2.1	11	7	82	57,800
	Macedonia	Skopje	25.7	2.1	0.2	12	9	76	12,800
	Madagascar	Antananarivo	587	23.8	2.6	33	7	66	1,400
	Malawi	Lilongwe	118	18.0	3.3	42	8	61	800
	Malaysia	Kuala Lumpur/ Putrajaya	330	30.5	1.4	20	5	75	24,100
	Mali	Bamako	1,240	17.0	3.0	45	13	55	1,500
	Malta	Valletta	0.3	0.4	0.3	10	9	80	27,000
	Mauritania	Nouakchott	1,026	3.6	2.2	31	8	63	3,700
	Mauritius	Port Louis	2.0	1.3	0.6	13	7	75	18,300
	Mexico	Mexico City	1,958	121.7	1.2	19	5	76	16,500
	Moldova	Kishinev	33.9	3.5	-1.0	12	13	70	5,500
	Mongolia	Ulan Bator	1,567	3.0	1.3	20	6	69	11,100
	Montenegro	Podgorica	14.0	0.6	-0.4	10	9	69	14,500
	Morocco	Rabat	447	33.3	1.0	18	5	77	7,100
	Mozambique	Maputo	802	25.3	2.5	39	12	53	1,100
	Namibia	Windhoek	824	2.2	0.6	20	14	52	9,700
	Nepal	Katmandu	147	31.6	1.8	21	7	68	2,400
	Netherlands	Amsterdam/ The Hague	41.5	16.9	0.4	11	9	81	47,700
	New Zealand	Wellington	271	4.4	0.8	13	7	81	33,800
	Nicaragua	Managua	130	5.9	1.0	18	5	73	4,800
	Niger	Niamey	1,267	18.0	3.3	45	12	55	900
	Nigeria	Abuja	924	181.6	2.5	38	13	53	5,700
	Norway	Oslo	324	5.2	1.1	12	8	82	66,000
	Oman	Muscat	310	3.3	2.1	24	3	75	33,700
	Pakistan	Islamabad	796	199.1	1.5	23	6	67	5,100
	Panama	Panamá	75.5	3.7	1.3	18	5	78	19,900
	Papua New Guinea	Port Moresby	463	6.7	1.8	24	7	67	2,500
	Paraguay	Asunción	407	6.8	1.2	16	5	77	8,500
	Peru	Lima	1,285	30.4	1.0	18	6	73	11,400
	Philippines	Manila	300	101.0	1.6	24	6	69	8,400
	Poland	Warsaw	323	38.6	-0.1	10	10	77	24,100
	Portugal	Lisbon	88.8	10.8	0.1	9	11	79	28,000
	Qatar	Doha	11.0	2.2	3.1	10	2	79	139,800

FLAG	COUNTRY	CAPITAL CITY	AREA thousand square kilometres 2015	POPULATION in millions 2015	POPULATION CHANGE percent per year 2015	BIRTHS per thousand people 2015	DEATHS per thousand people 2015	LIFE EXPECTANCY years 2015	INCOME US $ per person 2014
	Romania	Bucharest	238	21.7	-0.3	9	12	75	19,000
	Russia	Moscow	17,075	142.4	0.0	12	14	70	24,700
	Rwanda	Kigali	26.3	12.7	2.6	34	9	60	1,600
	Saudi Arabia	Riyadh	2,150	27.8	1.5	19	3	75	51,300
	Senegal	Dakar	197	14.0	2.5	35	8	61	2,300
	Serbia	Belgrade	77.5	7.2	-0.5	9	14	75	12,200
	Sierra Leone	Freetown	71.7	5.9	2.4	37	11	58	1,800
	Singapore	Singapore	0.7	5.7	1.9	8	3	85	80,300
	Slovakia	Bratislava	49.0	5.4	0.0	10	10	77	26,000
	Slovenia	Ljubljana	20.3	2.0	-0.3	8	11	78	28,700
	Solomon Islands	Honiara	28.9	0.6	2.0	26	4	75	2,000
	Somalia	Mogadishu	638	10.6	1.8	40	14	52	600
	South Africa	Cape Town/ Pretoria	1,221	53.7	1.3	21	10	62	12,700
	South Sudan	Juba	620	12.0	4.0	37	8	-	2,000
	Spain	Madrid	498	48.1	0.9	10	9	82	32,900
	Sri Lanka	Colombo	65.6	22.1	0.8	16	6	77	10,300
	Sudan	Khartoum	1,886	36.1	1.7	29	8	64	3,900
	Suriname	Paramaribo	163	0.6	1.1	16	6	72	16,100
	Swaziland	Mbabane	17.4	1.4	1.1	25	14	51	5,900
	Sweden	Stockholm	450	9.8	0.8	12	9	82	46,700
	Switzerland	Berne	41.3	8.1	0.7	11	8	83	59,600
	Syria	Damascus	185	17.1	-0.2	22	4	75	5,100
	Taiwan	Taipei	36.0	23.4	0.2	8	7	80	37,900
	Tajikistan	Dushanbe	143	8.2	1.7	24	6	67	2,700
	Tanzania	Dodoma	945	51.0	2.8	36	8	62	2,500
	Thailand	Bangkok	513	68.0	0.3	11	8	74	13,800
	Togo	Lomé	56.8	7.6	2.7	34	7	65	1,300
	Trinidad and Tobago	Port of Spain	5.1	1.2	-0.1	13	9	73	26,100
	Tunisia	Tunis	164	11.0	0.9	17	6	76	10,600
	Turkey	Ankara	775	79.4	1.3	16	6	75	19,000
	Turkmenistan	Ashkhabad	488	5.2	1.1	19	6	70	14,500
	Uganda	Kampala	241	37.1	3.2	44	11	55	1,700
	Ukraine	Kiev	604	44.4	-0.6	11	14	72	8,600
	United Arab Emirates	Abu Dhabi	83.6	5.8	2.6	15	2	77	66,300
	United Kingdom	London	242	64.1	0.5	12	9	81	38,400
	USA	Washington D.C.	9,629	321.4	0.8	12	8	80	55,900
	Uruguay	Montevideo	175	3.3	0.3	13	9	77	20,200
	Uzbekistan	Tashkent	447	29.2	0.9	17	5	74	5,800
	Venezuela	Caracas	912	29.3	1.4	19	5	75	17,200
	Vietnam	Hanoi	332	94.3	1.0	16	6	73	5,400
	Yemen	Sana	528	26.7	2.5	30	6	65	3,700
	Zambia	Lusaka	753	15.1	2.9	42	13	52	3,700
	Zimbabwe	Harare	391	14.2	2.2	32	10	57	1,600

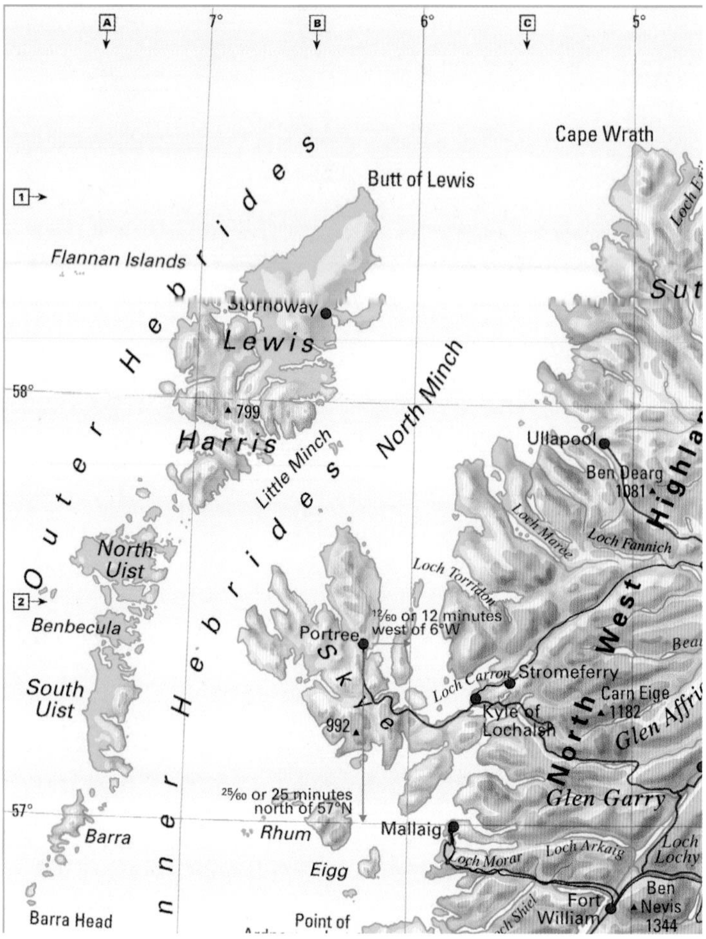

This index contains the names of all the principal places and features shown on the maps in the atlas. They are listed in alphabetical order. If a name has a description as part of it, for example, Bay of Biscay, the name is in alphabetical order, followed by the description:

Biscay, Bay of . . . . . .

Sometimes, the same name occurs in more than one country. In these cases, the country names are added after each place name. For example:

Córdoba, *Argentina* . .
Córdoba, *Spain* . . . . .

All rivers are indexed to their mouths or confluences and are followed by the symbol →. All country names are followed by the symbol ■.

Each place name is followed by its latitude and longitude, and then its map page number and figure-letter grid reference. Both latitude and longitude are measured in degrees and minutes. There are 60 minutes in a degree. The latitude is followed by N(orth) or S(outh) and the longitude by E(ast) or W(est). The map extract on the left shows how to find a place by estimating the required distance from the nearest line of latitude or longitude on the map page. Portree is used as an example:

Portree . . . . 57°25'N 6°12'W **18 2B**

There are 60 minutes between the lines and so to find the position of Portree an estimate has to be made. 25 parts of the 60 minutes north of the 57°N latitude line, and 12 parts of the 60 minutes west of the 6°W longitude line.

The latitude and longitude are followed by a number in bold type which refers to the number of the map page on which the place or feature appears. Portree is on page **18**.

The figure and letter which follow the page number give the grid rectangle on the map within which the place or feature appears. The grid is formed by the lines of latitude and longitude. The columns are labelled at the top and bottom of the map with a letter and the rows at the sides of the map with a number. Portree is in the grid square where row **2** crosses column **B**.

A

Aalborg	57° 2'N	9°54' E	**32**	**4N**
Aarhus	56° 8'N	10°11' E	**32**	**4P**
Aba	5°10'N	7°19' E	**52**	**2C**
Ābādān	30°22'N	48°20' E	**48**	**3E**
Abakan	53°40'N	91°10' E	**41**	**4K**
ABC Islands	12°15'N	69° 0'W	**67**	**6L**
Abeokuta	7° 3'N	3°19' E	**52**	**2B**
Aberdare	51°43'N	3°27'W	**17**	**5C**
Aberdare Range	0°15'S	36°50' E	**53**	**3B**
Aberdeen	57° 9'N	2° 5'W	**18**	**2F**
Abergavenny	51°49'N	3° 1'W	**17**	**5C**
Aberystwyth	52°25'N	4° 5'W	**17**	**4B**
Abidjan	5°26'N	3°58'W	**51**	**5B**
Abu Dhabi	24°28'N	54°22' E	**48**	**5F**
Abuja	9° 5'N	7°32' E	**52**	**2C**
Acapulco	16°51'N	99°55'W	**62**	**4D**
Accra	5°35'N	0° 6'W	**52**	**2A**
Accrington	53°45'N	2°22'W	**16**	**3D**
Achill Island	53°58'N	10° 1'W	**19**	**3A**
Aconcagua	32°39'S	70° 0'W	**64**	**7D**
Acre	9° 1'S	71° 0'W	**66**	**4A**
Ad Dammām	26°20'N	50° 5' E	**48**	**4F**
Adamawa Highlands	7°20'N	12°20' E	**52**	**2D**
Adana	37° 0'N	35°16' E	**35**	**4L**
Adare, Cape	71° 0'S	171° 0' E	**67**	**11E**
Addis Ababa	9° 2'N	38°42' E	**51**	**5F**
Adelaide	34°52'S	138°30' E	**54**	**8G**
Adelaide Island	67°15'S	68°30'W	**67**	**17D**
Adélie Land	68° 0'S	140° 0' E	**67**	**10D**
Aden	12°45'N	45° 0' E	**46**	**5C**
Aden, Gulf of	12°30'N	47°30' E	**46**	**5C**
Adriatic Sea	43° 0'N	16° 0' E	**36**	**3F**
Ægean Sea	38°30'N	25° 0' E	**35**	**4J**
Aeolian Islands	38°30'N	14°57' E	**36**	**5E**
Afghanistan ■	33° 0'N	65° 0' E	**46**	**3E**
Africa	10° 0'N	20° 0' E	**50**	**5E**
Agra	27°17'N	77°58' E	**46**	**4F**
Aguascalientes	21°53'N	102°18'W	**62**	**3D**
Ahmadabad	23° 0'N	72°40' E	**46**	**4F**
Ahvāz	31°20'N	48°40' E	**48**	**3E**
Ailsa Craig	55°15'N	5° 6'W	**18**	**4C**
Aïr	18°30'N	8° 0' E	**50**	**4C**
Airdrie	55°52'N	3°57'W	**18**	**4E**
Aire →	53°43'N	0°55'W	**13**	**5F**
Aix-en-Provence	43°32'N	5°27' E	**33**	**11L**
Ajaccio	41°55'N	8°40' E	**33**	**12N**
Akita	39°45'N	140° 7' E	**45**	**3D**
Akosombo Dam	6°20'N	0° 5' E	**52**	**2B**
Akron	41° 5'N	81°31'W	**59**	**2K**
Aksu	41° 5'N	80°10' E	**42**	**2C**
Al 'Ayn	24°15'N	55°45' E	**48**	**5G**
Al Aziziyah	32°30'N	13° 1' E	**34**	**5F**
Al Ḩillah	32°30'N	44°25' E	**48**	**3D**
Al Hufūf	25°25'N	49°45' E	**48**	**4E**
Al Jubayl	27° 0'N	49°50' E	**48**	**4E**
Al Kūt	32°30'N	46° 0' E	**48**	**3E**
Al Mubarraz	25°30'N	49°40' E	**48**	**4E**
Alabama	33° 0'N	87° 0'W	**59**	**4J**
Alabama →	31° 8'N	87°57'W	**59**	**4J**
Alagoas	9° 0'S	36° 0'W	**66**	**4H**
Åland Islands	60°15'N	20° 0' E	**31**	**3D**
Alaska	64° 0'N	154° 0'W	**57**	**3D**
Alaska, Gulf of	58° 0'N	145° 0'W	**56**	**4E**
Alaska Peninsula	56° 0'N	159° 0'W	**56**	**4D**
Alaska Range	62°50'N	151° 0'W	**56**	**3D**
Albacete	39° 0'N	1°50'W	**33**	**13H**
Albania ■	41° 0'N	20° 0' E	**35**	**3G**
Albany, *Australia*	35° 1'S	117°58' E	**54**	**9C**
Albany, *U.S.A.*	42°39'N	73°45'W	**59**	**2M**
Albuquerque	35° 5'N	106°39'W	**58**	**3E**
Aldabra Islands	9°22'S	46°28' E	**51**	**6G**
Aldeburgh	52°10'N	1°37' E	**17**	**4H**
Alderney	49°42'N	2°11'W	**17**	**7D**
Aleppo	36°10'N	37°15' E	**48**	**2C**
Ålesund	62°28'N	6°12' E	**31**	**3B**
Aleutian Islands	52° 0'N	175° 0'W	**68**	**2A**
Alexander Island	69° 0'S	70° 0'W	**67**	**17D**
Alexandria	31°13'N	29°58' E	**48**	**3A**
Algarve	36°58'N	8°20'W	**33**	**14D**
Algeria ■	28°30'N	2° 0' E	**51**	**3C**
Algiers	36°42'N	3° 8' E	**51**	**2C**
Alicante	38°23'N	0°30'W	**33**	**13H**
Alice Springs	23°40'S	133°50' E	**54**	**6F**
Allahabad	25°25'N	81°58' E	**46**	**4G**
Allegheny Mountains	38°15'N	80°10'W	**59**	**3L**
Allen, Bog of	53°15'N	7° 0'W	**19**	**3D**
Allen, Lough	54° 8'N	8° 4'W	**19**	**2C**
Alloa	56° 7'N	3°47'W	**18**	**3E**
Alma Ata	43°15'N	76°57' E	**40**	**5H**
Almería	36°52'N	2°27'W	**33**	**14G**
Alness	57°41'N	4°16'W	**18**	**2D**
Alnwick	55°24'N	1°42'W	**16**	**1E**
Alps	46°30'N	9°30' E	**33**	**9N**
Altai	46°40'N	92°45' E	**40**	**4J**
Altay	47°48'N	88°10' E	**42**	**2C**
Altun Shan	38°30'N	88° 0' E	**42**	**3C**
Amapá	1°40'N	52° 0'W	**66**	**2E**
Amarillo	35°13'N	101°50'W	**58**	**3F**
Amazon →	0° 5'S	50° 0'W	**66**	**3E**
Amazonas	5° 0'S	65° 0'W	**66**	**4B**
Ambon	3°43'S	128°12' E	**47**	**7L**
American Highland	73° 0'S	75° 0' E	**67**	**6E**
American Samoa	14°20'S	170° 0'W	**55**	**4S**
Amery Ice Shelf	69°30'S	72° 0' E	**67**	**6D**
Amiens	49°54'N	2°16' E	**33**	**8J**
Amlwch	53°24'N	4°20'W	**16**	**3B**
'Ammān	31°57'N	35°52' E	**48**	**3C**
Amritsar	31°35'N	74°57' E	**46**	**3F**
Amsterdam	52°23'N	4°54' E	**32**	**6L**
Amudarya →	43°58'N	59°34' E	**40**	**5F**
Amundsen Sea	72° 0'S	115° 0'W	**67**	**15E**
Amur →	52°56'N	141°10' E	**41**	**4Q**
An Najaf	32° 3'N	44°15' E	**48**	**3D**
An Nāşirīyah	31° 0'N	46°15' E	**48**	**3E**
Anápolis	16°15'S	48°50'W	**66**	**6F**
Anatolia	39° 0'N	30° 0' E	**48**	**2B**
Anchorage	61°13'N	149°54'W	**57**	**3E**
Ancona	43°38'N	13°30' E	**36**	**3D**
Andalucía	37°35'N	5° 0'W	**33**	**14F**
Andaman Islands	12°30'N	92°45' E	**46**	**5H**
Andaman Sea	13° 0'N	96° 0' E	**38**	**7L**
Andes	10° 0'S	75°53'W	**64**	**5D**
Andizhan	41°10'N	72°15' E	**42**	**2B**
Andorra ■	42°30'N	1°30' E	**33**	**11J**
Andover	51°12'N	1°29'W	**17**	**5E**
Aneto, Pico de	42°37'N	0°40' E	**33**	**11J**
Angara →	58° 5'N	94°20' E	**41**	**4K**
Angel Falls	5°57'N	62°30'W	**63**	**6M**
Angers	47°30'N	0°35'W	**33**	**9H**
Anglesey	53°17'N	4°20'W	**16**	**3B**
Angola ■	12° 0'S	18° 0' E	**51**	**7D**
Angoulême	45°39'N	0°10' E	**33**	**10J**
Angus	56°46'N	2°56'W	**15**	**3E**
Ankara	39°57'N	32°54' E	**35**	**4K**
Annaba	36°50'N	7°46' E	**34**	**4E**
Annan	54°59'N	3°16'W	**18**	**5E**
Annan →	54°58'N	3°16'W	**18**	**4E**
Annapolis	38°59'N	76°30'W	**59**	**3L**
Annobón	1°25'S	5°36' E	**50**	**6C**
Anshan	41° 5'N	122°58' E	**43**	**2G**
Antalya	36°52'N	30°45' E	**35**	**4K**
Antananarivo	18°55'S	47°31' E	**51**	**7G**
Antarctic Peninsula	67° 0'S	60° 0'W	**67**	**18D**
Antarctica	90° 0'S	0° 0'W	**67**	**3F**
Antigua & Barbuda ■	17°20'N	61°48'W	**63**	**4M**
Antofagasta	23°50'S	70°30'W	**65**	**6D**
Antrim	54°43'N	6°14'W	**19**	**2E**
Antrim, Mountains of	55° 3'N	6°14'W	**19**	**2E**
Antwerp	51°13'N	4°25' E	**32**	**7L**
Anvers Island	64°30'S	63°40'W	**67**	**17D**
Aomori	40°45'N	140°45' E	**45**	**2D**
Aoraki Mount Cook	43°36'S	170° 9' E	**55**	**10P**
Apennines	44°30'N	10° 0' E	**36**	**3D**
Apia	13°50'S	171°50'W	**55**	**4S**
Appalachian Mountains	38° 0'N	80° 0'W	**59**	**3K**
Appleby-in-Westmorland	54°35'N	2°29'W	**16**	**2D**
Aqaba	29°31'N	35° 0' E	**48**	**4C**
Arabia	25° 0'N	45° 0' E	**38**	**6F**
Arabian Sea	16° 0'N	65° 0' E	**46**	**5E**
Aracaju	10°55'S	37° 4'W	**66**	**5H**
Araçatuba	21°10'S	50°30'W	**66**	**7E**
Araguaia →	5°21'S	48°41'W	**66**	**4F**
Arāk	34° 0'N	49°40' E	**48**	**3E**
Araks →	40° 5'N	48°29' E	**48**	**1E**
Aral Sea	45° 0'N	58°20' E	**40**	**5F**
Aran Islands	53° 6'N	9°38'W	**19**	**3B**
Ararat, Mount	39°50'N	44°15' E	**48**	**2D**
Arbroath	56°34'N	2°35'W	**18**	**3F**
Arctic Ocean	78° 0'N	160° 0'W	**67**	**18B**
Ardabīl	38°15'N	48°18' E	**48**	**2E**
Ardnamurchan, Point of	56°43'N	6°14'W	**18**	**3B**
Ardrossan	55°39'N	4°49'W	**18**	**4D**
Ards Peninsula	54°33'N	5°34'W	**19**	**2F**
Arequipa	16°20'S	71°30'W	**65**	**5D**
Argentina ■	35° 0'S	66° 0'W	**65**	**7E**
Argun →	53°20'N	121°28' E	**43**	**1F**
Argyle, Lake	16°20'S	128°40' E	**54**	**5E**
Argyll	56°10'N	5°20'W	**18**	**3C**
Argyll & Bute	56°13'N	5°28'W	**15**	**3D**
Arica	18°32'S	70°20'W	**65**	**5D**
Aripuanā →	5° 7'S	60°25'W	**66**	**4C**
Arizona	34° 0'N	112° 0'W	**58**	**4D**
Arkaig, Loch	56°59'N	5°10'W	**18**	**3C**
Arkansas	35° 0'N	92°30'W	**59**	**4H**
Arkansas →	33°47'N	91° 4'W	**59**	**4H**
Arkhangelsk	64°38'N	40°36' E	**31**	**3J**
Arklow	52°48'N	6°10'W	**19**	**4E**
Armagh	54°21'N	6°39'W	**19**	**2E**
Armenia ■	40°20'N	45° 0' E	**48**	**1D**
Arnhem	51°58'N	5°55' E	**32**	**7L**
Arnhem Land	13°10'S	134°30' E	**54**	**4F**
Arran	55°34'N	5°12'W	**18**	**4C**
Arranmore	55° 0'N	8°30'W	**19**	**1C**
Aru Islands	6° 0'S	134°30' E	**47**	**7M**
Aruba	12°30'N	70° 0'W	**63**	**5L**
Arusha	3°20'S	36°40' E	**53**	**3B**
Arvayheer	46°15'N	102°48' E	**42**	**2E**
As Sulaymānīyah, *Iraq*	35°35'N	45°29' E	**48**	**2E**
As Sulaymānīyah, *Saudi Arabia*	24° 9'N	47°18' E	**48**	**5E**
Asahikawa	43°46'N	142°22' E	**45**	**2D**
Asamankese	5°50'N	0°40'W	**52**	**2A**
Ascension Island	7°57'S	14°23'W	**51**	**6A**
Ashford	51° 8'N	0°53' E	**17**	**5G**
Ashington	55°11'N	1°33'W	**16**	**1E**
Ashkhabad	37°58'N	58°24' E	**48**	**2G**
Ashton under Lyne	53°29'N	2° 6'W	**16**	**3D**
Asmara	15°19'N	38°55' E	**51**	**4F**
Assam	26° 0'N	93° 0' E	**46**	**4H**
Astana	51°10'N	71°30' E	**40**	**4H**
Astrakhan	46°25'N	48° 5' E	**38**	**5E**
Asunción	25°10'S	57°30'W	**65**	**6F**
Aswân	24° 4'N	32°57' E	**48**	**5B**
Asyût	27°11'N	31° 4' E	**48**	**4B**
Aţ Ţā'if	21° 5'N	40°27' E	**48**	**5D**
Atacama Desert	24° 0'S	69°20'W	**64**	**6E**
Athens	37°58'N	23°43' E	**35**	**4H**
Athlone	53°25'N	7°56'W	**19**	**3D**
Athy	53° 0'N	7° 0'W	**19**	**4E**
Atlanta	33°45'N	84°23'W	**59**	**4K**
Atlantic Ocean	0° 0'	20° 0'W	**68**	**3G**
Atlas Mountains	32°30'N	5° 0'W	**50**	**2B**
Auckland	36°52'S	174°46' E	**55**	**9P**
Augsburg	48°25'N	10°52' E	**33**	**8P**
Augusta	44°19'N	69°47'W	**59**	**2N**
Austin	30°17'N	97°45'W	**58**	**4G**
Australia ■	23° 0'S	135° 0' E	**54**	**6D**
Australian Capital Territory (A.C.T.)	35°30'S	149° 0' E	**54**	**9J**
Austria ■	47° 0'N	14° 0' E	**34**	**2F**
Aviemore	57°12'N	3°50'W	**18**	**2E**
Avignon	43°57'N	4°50' E	**33**	**11L**
Avon →, *Bristol*	51°29'N	2°41'W	**17**	**5D**
Avon →, *Dorset*	50°44'N	1°46'W	**17**	**6E**
Avon →, *Warwickshire*	52° 0'N	2° 8'W	**17**	**4D**
Awe, Loch	56°17'N	5°16'W	**18**	**3C**
Ayers Rock = Uluru	25°23'S	131° 5' E	**54**	**7F**
Aylesbury	51°49'N	0°49'W	**17**	**5F**
Ayr	55°28'N	4°38'W	**18**	**4D**
Azerbaijan ■	40°20'N	48° 0' E	**48**	**1E**
Azores	38° 0'N	27° 0'W	**68**	**3H**
Azov, Sea of	46° 0'N	36°30' E	**35**	**2L**